Facts and Folklore about the U.S.A.

Stars and Stripes

Pamela McPartland-Fairman, Ph. D.

Boston   Burr Ridge, IL   Dubuque, IA   Madison, WI   New York   San Francisco   St. Louis
Bangkok   Bogotá   Caracas   Lisbon   London   Madrid
Mexico City   Milan   New Delhi   Seoul   Singapore   Sydney   Taipei   Toronto

McGraw-Hill

*A Division of The **McGraw·Hill** Companies*

Stars and Stripes
Facts and Folklore about the U.S.A.

This book is printed on acid-free paper.

domestic   2 3 4 5 6 7 8 9 0 QPD QPD 3 2 1 0
international   1 2 3 4 5 6 7 8 9 0 QPD QPD 3 2 1 0

ISBN 0-07-045993-2

Editorial Director: Thalia Dorwick
Publisher: Tim Stookesberry
Developmental editor: Pam Tiberia
Marketing manager: Tracy Landrum
Project manager: Michelle Munn
Production supervisor: Richard DeVitto
Designer: Vargas/Williams Design
Cover designer: Bradley Thomas
Art editor: Nicole Widmyer
Illustrators: Allan Eitzen, Lori Heckelman, Edie Williams
Editorial Assistant: Bridget Terry
Compositor: Clarinda Company
Typeface: Century Schoolbook
Printer: Quebecor Press Dubuque

Grateful acknowledgment is made for use of the following:
Page 1 (bottom left) Buddy Mays/Corbis, *(bottom right)* © The Andy Warhol Foundation/Art Resource, NY; *2 (left)* Culver Pictures Inc.; *10 (bottom left)* © The Andy Warhol Foundation/Art Resource, NY, *(bottom right)* © AP/Wide World Photo; *21* © Buddy Mays/Corbis; *22 (clockwise from top left)* © Frederic Remington Art Museum, © Paul Souders/Corbis, © Hulton Getty/Tony Stone Images, © Patrick Ward/Corbis; *27 (top)* ©1998 The Museum of Modern Art, New York, *(bottom right)* © Stock Montage; *28 (bottom from left)* Courtesy National Library of Congress, © Ken Biggs/Tony Stone Images, © Hulton Getty/Tony Stone Images, © Martin Barraud/Tony Stone Images, Courtesy National Library of Congress; *32 (clockwise from left)* © Robert Kusel/Tony Stone Images, Courtesy of Kraft Foods, Inc., © 1998 The Museum of Modern Art, New York; *36 (top left)* © AP/Wide World Photo, *(top right)* Culver Picture Inc.; *38 (bottom)* © Hulton-Deutsch/Corbis; *43 (left)* © James Blair/Corbis, *(second from right)* © Rafael Macia/Photo Researchers, Inc.; *44 (top right)* © Stock Montage, *(bottom right)* © Culver Picture Inc.; *46* Courtesy National Library of Congress; *53 (top)* © Culver Picture Archive, *(bottom right)* © Tom Neiman/Stock Montage, Inc.; *62 (clockwise from top left)* © Corbis-Bettmann, © Sandy Felsenthal/Corbis, Courtesy Jeffery Howe, © Joe Demaio/City of Madison, © Angelo Hornack/Corbis, © Hulton Getty/Tony Stone Images; *65* Courtesy Kankakee County Historical Society; *68 (clockwise from top left)* © Michael Yamashita/Corbis, © Tom Neiman/Stock Montage, Inc., © Joseph Sohm/Corbis, © Rafael Macia/Photo Researchers, inc., © Peter Pearson/Tony Stone Images, © Robert Holms/Corbis; *79 (clockwise from top left)* © Hulton Getty/Tony Stone Images, © Culver Picture Archive, © David M. Grossman/Photo Researchers, Inc.; *84 (from left)* © Hulton Getty/Tony Stone Images, © AP/Wide World Photo, © UPI/Corbis; *88* © Hulton Getty/Tony Stone Images; *92 (left)* © David M. Grossman/Photo Researchers, Inc., *(right)* © Brooks Kraft/Sygma. All other photographs courtesy of Huck Fairman.

http://www.mhhe.com

Contents

Preface

Stars and Stripes is a reading, writing, listening, and discussion book for low-intermediate to intermediate ESOL students. The core of the text is a collection of stories about the United States—its history and culture, past and present. The text is organized into four units, each containing three chapters. The units are: Popular Culture; Symbols; Education, Architecture, and Music; and History. Each chapter offers two readings, one dealing with the past, followed by a related reading from the present. At the end of each chapter, a section called Just the Facts provides additional information which students can incorporate in their discussions.

Stars and Stripes evolves and develops with the learner. Readings are shorter and easier in early chapters, gradually building in length and complexity as the text progresses. Activities also become more varied and demanding. For example, students are initially asked to choose the best summary of a given story; later, they are asked to write their own summary. Similarly, in early chapters, students are directed to match pictures with paragraphs of a story; in later chapters, they use details from the reading to write captions for pictures.

 For students and teachers who would like to listen to the readings, a 45-minute audiocassette is available. Students may choose to listen to the audiocassette on their own, or the instructor can play the cassette while students read the passage in class or when they do the exercise Read in Groups of Words.

Language-learning strategies—such as checking comprehension with a partner, and reading groups of words instead of word-by-word—are included throughout the text to help students look at their own learning process and build a repertoire of ways to become active learners, both during and after the course.

In Stars and Stripes, reading is integrated with writing, listening, and speaking. Here are some of the activities students will do:

Before reading:

- discuss the topic
- interview their classmates
- review what they already know about the topic
- take a quiz about the topic
- predict the content of the reading based on pictures

While reading:

- match pictures with paragraphs
- mark the text for the topic or main idea
- find evidence for a particular point of view
- look for answers to the pre-reading quiz
- take notes or make an outline
- write captions for pictures

After reading:

- react to the passage
- check their predictions

- pick a title for the reading
- put sentences in order
- identify facts *vs.* opinions, and stated *vs.* implied information
- make a time line
- use words from the reading to complete a conversation
- compare issues cross-culturally
- figure out the meaning of words from the context
- write or correct a summary
- look for examples that support a point

These activities help students make sense of the readings, and then encourage them to use details from the readings to discuss contemporary issues. Almost all of the activities involve either pair- or group-work, thus maximizing student-to-student interaction. When students work alone on an activity, they follow up by comparing answers with a partner. Thus, students have numerous opportunities to communicate in meaningful ways in a collaborative atmosphere.

A review page at the end of each unit gives students a chance to identify those activities which were most helpful, and provides an opportunity to reexamine some of the details presented in that unit. Unit reviews also offer suggestions for further research, reading, and video viewing, so students can extend learning beyond the classroom.

Acknowledgments

Family, friends, and colleagues have contributed to this project in direct and indirect ways, and I thank them all. For lively discussions of content-based learning, I thank Kate Garretson of Kingsborough Community College, CUNY. While collaborating on *Connect With English* with Karen Price of Harvard University's Graduate School of Education, I learned, among other things, the importance of building contemporary, cultural issues into my ESOL materials. Tim Stookesberry saw the promise of this text and brought it to McGraw-Hill. He also solved a number of problems during the editing process. Michelle Munn and Nicole Widmyer of McGraw-Hill ably and calmly acquired and organized the photographs, maps, and drawings in the book. John Chapman provided support and editorial help with an early draft, and Bill Preston and Pam Tiberia of McGraw-Hill offered numerous suggestions while editing the final version. My husband, Huck Fairman, helped on a day-to-day basis by discussing the topics, tightening the stories, and taking some of the photographs.

Popular Culture

Did You Know . . . ?
- Americans receive about thirty greeting cards a year.
- A typical girl in the United States owns eight Barbie dolls.
- There are over 800 rodeos a year in the United States.

In Unit One, you will learn about some of the things people in the United States do in their free time: select and send greeting cards, collect and play with Barbie dolls, and go to rodeos and cowboy museums.

Part One
Greeting Cards

Before You Read

1. Interview First, write your own answers to the following survey questions. Then interview your partner and write his or her answers. Discuss answers with your partner.

Greeting Card Survey

MY ANSWERS:	MY PARTNER'S ANSWERS:
1. Do you buy greeting cards? ☐ yes ☐ no	**1.** Do you buy greeting cards? ☐ yes ☐ no
2. Do you write a note or send something with your cards? ☐ yes ☐ no	**2.** Do you write a note or send something with your cards? ☐ yes ☐ no
3. How many cards do you get a year? ☐ 0–19 ☐ 20–29 ☐ 30+	**3.** How many cards do you get a year? ☐ 0–19 ☐ 20–29 ☐ 30+
4. How many birthday cards do you get? ☐ 0–4 ☐ 5–9 ☐ 10+	**4.** How many birthday cards do you get? ☐ 0–4 ☐ 5–9 ☐ 10+

While You Read

2. Match Drawings and Paragraphs Match each paragraph of the reading on page 3 with one of the pictures below. Compare answers with a partner.

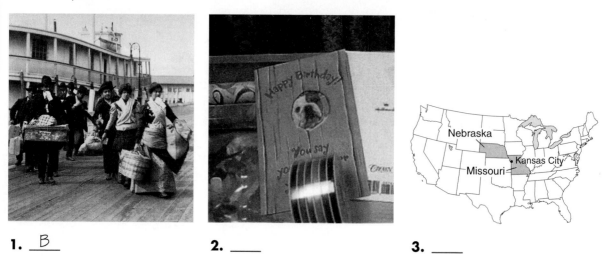

1. _B_

2. ____

3. ____

A   In the early 1900s, the Hall brothers owned a gift shop in a small town in Nebraska. Business wasn't very good, so, in 1910, one of the brothers moved east to Kansas City, Missouri. He took several boxes of postcards with him and set up a card shop there. This was the beginning of the greeting card company called Hall Brothers.

B   The company grew for several reasons. First, the U.S. population increased rapidly at the beginning of the twentieth century. This increase was partly because of the arrival of large numbers of immigrants from Eastern and Southern Europe. Second, literacy was spreading—in other words, more Americans learned to read and write. Third, people in the U.S. moved frequently. They needed a simple way to stay in touch with friends and family. The easiest way to communicate was to send a card.

C   In 1954, the company changed its name from Hall Brothers to Hallmark. (A "hallmark" is a sign of good quality.) The company changed in other ways, too. It began to manufacture new products. These included wrapping paper, ribbon, paper plates, napkins, photo albums, and other gifts. But Hallmark is most famous for its greeting cards. It prints over ten million of them every day. In fact, the name, Hallmark, is synonymous with greeting cards. And the company is still based in Kansas City, Missouri.

After You Read

3. Read in Groups of Words

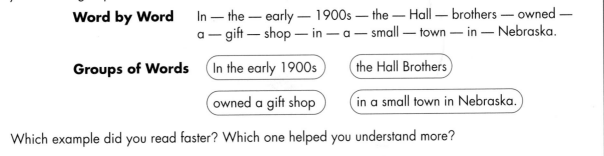

Reading Strategy

Most people read word by word in a new language. But you can read faster and understand more if you read in *groups* of words. Read the two examples below.

Word by Word   In — the — early — 1900s — the — Hall — brothers — owned — a — gift — shop — in — a — small — town — in — Nebraska.

Groups of Words   (In the early 1900s)   (the Hall Brothers)

(owned a gift shop)   (in a small town in Nebraska.)

Which example did you read faster? Which one helped you understand more?

Listen as your teacher reads the story in groups of words. Circle each group you hear.
Then read the story again silently.

4. Match Topics and Paragraphs Match each of the following topics with a paragraph from the reading. Write the letters of the paragraphs on the lines. Compare answers with a partner.

_____ **1.** why Hall Brothers grew

_____ **2.** how Hallmark has changed and what it's famous for today

_____ **3.** how the company called Hall Brothers began

5. Pick a Title Work with a partner. Pick another title for the reading. Check one of the following boxes. The title gives the subject of the reading.

☐ **1.** A Gift Shop in Nebraska

☐ **2.** The History of Hallmark

☐ **3.** The Hall Brothers

Discuss why the other two are not good titles.

6. Connect Nouns and Pronouns In the paragraph below, the circled words are pronouns. They refer to other words (nouns or noun phrases) in the paragraph. Underline the words that the pronouns refer to, and draw lines to connect them. Compare answers with a partner.

The company changed in other ways, too. It[1] began to manufacture new products. These[2] included wrapping paper, ribbon, paper plates, napkins, photo albums, and other gifts. But Hallmark is most famous for its greeting cards. It[3] prints over 10 million of them[4] every day.

7. Put Sentences in Order Work with a partner. Number the following sentences in the correct order from 1 to 6. Then close your book and try to tell your partner the sentences in order.

_____ Hallmark produces over 10 million cards each day.

__1__ The company called Hall Brothers grew quickly.

_____ The Hall brothers owned a gift shop in Nebraska.

_____ Hall Brothers became Hallmark.

_____ One brother left Nebraska and set up a card shop in Missouri.

_____ The company began to make new products but was still famous for its cards.

8. Complete the Conversation   Use words from the box to complete the conversation. Compare answers with a partner.

> keep in touch
> postcards
> ribbon
> ✓shop
> wrapping

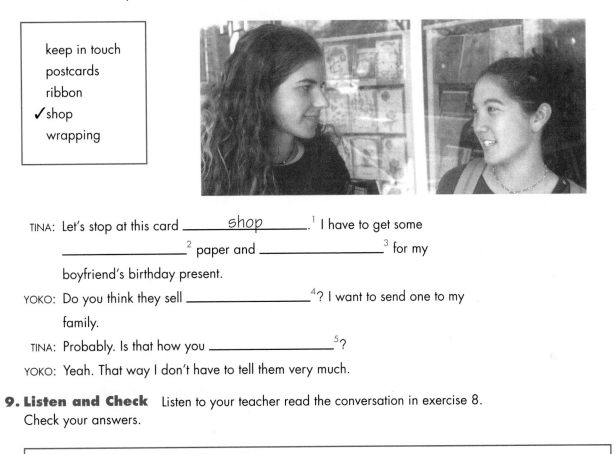

TINA: Let's stop at this card _____shop_____.¹ I have to get some
_____² paper and _____³ for my
boyfriend's birthday present.

YOKO: Do you think they sell _____⁴? I want to send one to my
family.

TINA: Probably. Is that how you _____⁵?

YOKO: Yeah. That way I don't have to tell them very much.

9. Listen and Check   Listen to your teacher read the conversation in exercise 8.
Check your answers.

Listening Strategy
If you want to be sure of an answer, you can say: "Excuse me, did you say *shop*?"

---

10. Write and Discuss   On a separate sheet of paper, write your answers to the
following questions. Then discuss your opinions in small groups.

1.   Do you think it's better to write letters or send cards? Why?
2.   Do you think electronic mail (e-mail) will be good or bad for the greeting card business? Why?
3.   First there was Mother's Day and Father's Day. Then in 1978, there was Grandparents Day. Card
companies want more holidays like Grandparents Day so they can sell more cards and gifts. Some
people call these days *Hallmark Holidays*. What do you think of Hallmark Holidays?

Part Two

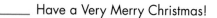

Cards for Every Day

Before You Read

1. Match Cards and Messages   Work with a partner. Match the following messages with the greeting cards.

_____ Be My Valentine!

_____ Is he husband number 3 or 4?

_____ Have a Very Merry Christmas!

_____ You're 20 with 30 years of experience. Happy Birthday!

1.

2.

3.

4.

While You Read

2. Mark the Text   In the reading on page 7, mark anything that's new or surprising to you by writing "new" in the margin to the left of it. Then compare what you marked with a partner.

A   Americans love greeting cards. Each year, people in the United States buy more than seven billion cards. The three most popular kinds of cards are those for special occasions: Christmas, birthdays, and Valentine's Day (a day for sweethearts to exchange cards and gifts, celebrated on February 14).

B   Traditional cards are very simple. They present a beautiful picture on the cover and cheerful words inside. Some cards, however, are more complex. They can have a strange photograph on the outside and a funny joke inside. Some birthday cards play an electronic musical message, and some Valentine's Day cards fill the air with perfume.

C   Cards change with a changing society. For example, anniversary cards are no longer just for "Mom and Dad." Because of the high rate of divorce and second marriages in the United States, there are now anniversary cards for "Mom and her husband" and "Dad and his wife." Also, cards are no longer just for special occasions. Now there are cards for the person who lost a job, lost a game, or lost some weight.

D   Today, Hallmark is one of 1,500 companies that produce greeting cards in the United States. But why do Americans send so many cards? Modern life leaves little time to write to friends and relatives. A card takes less time than a letter and is usually cheaper than a phone call. For many people, cards offer a quick and easy way to stay in touch.

After You Read

3. Look for Examples   Good writing often includes examples to support the main ideas. Read the following main ideas. Then find at least one example in the reading to support each idea. Compare answers with a partner.

1.   Americans love greeting cards: _____

_____

2.   Some cards are simple, but others are more complex: _____

_____

3.   Cards change with a changing society: _____

_____

4. Pick the Summary   Read the following summaries. Then check the one that best summarizes the reading. Compare answers with a partner.

☐ **1.** Hallmark continues to be one of the biggest greeting card companies in the United States, but it is now one of 1,500 companies. It has changed as society has changed.

☐ **2.** Americans use cards as a quick and easy way to communicate with friends and family. Today, cards are not just for special occasions like birthdays, Christmas, and Valentine's Day. They also celebrate second marriages and many other events.

☐ **3.** Christmas (December 25) is the holiday for which Americans buy the most cards. It is a time for people to write a note and send family photos to relatives and friends they haven't seen all year. Some Americans even type a long letter with details about each family member and send it with their Christmas greetings.

5. Match Cards and Events   Work with a partner. Match each event in the left column with the appropriate card on the right.

EVENTS		CARDS
____ **1.** the day two people were married	✓**a.**	a Mother's Day card
____ **2.** the day a person was born	**b.**	a Father's Day card
_a_ **3.** the second Sunday in May	**c.**	a sympathy card
____ **4.** a death in a friend's family	**d.**	an anniversary card
____ **5.** the third Sunday in June	**e.**	a birthday card

6. Make a Card   Think about someone you need to send a card to. Is it the person's birthday? Is it a special occasion? The list of cards in Exercise 5 may help you decide. Draw a cover for your card and write a message inside. Use the space below to practice. Then, make your card on a separate piece of paper and mail it.

The cover: Your message:

7. Complete the Conversation Use words from the box to complete the conversation. Compare answers with a partner.

buy
✓ cover
messages
photographs
produce
quick

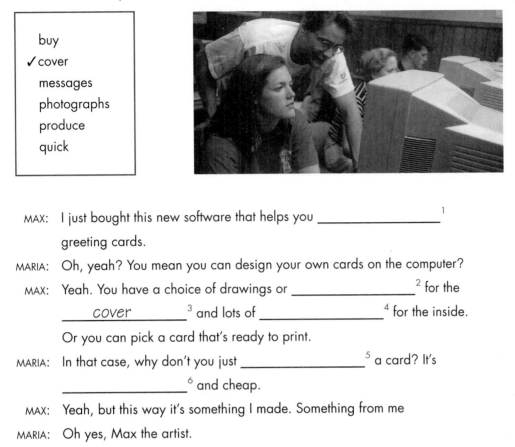

MAX: I just bought this new software that helps you _____ [1] greeting cards.

MARIA: Oh, yeah? You mean you can design your own cards on the computer?

MAX: Yeah. You have a choice of drawings or _____ [2] for the ____cover____ [3] and lots of _____ [4] for the inside. Or you can pick a card that's ready to print.

MARIA: In that case, why don't you just _____ [5] a card? It's _____ [6] and cheap.

MAX: Yeah, but this way it's something I made. Something from me

MARIA: Oh yes, Max the artist.

8. Write and Discuss Read **Just the Facts**. Then read the questions that follow and write your answers on a separate sheet of paper. Discuss your answers in small groups.

Just the Facts: Greeting Card Customs in the United States

- Women buy about 85 to 90 percent of all greeting cards.
- 83 percent of Americans write a note or send something (a photo or newspaper clipping) with their cards.
- The typical American receives about thirty greeting cards a year.
- The typical American receives about eight cards on his or her birthday.

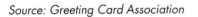

Source: Greeting Card Association

1. Compare the facts above with your answers to the Greeting Card Survey on page 2. Are you similar to the typical American or completely different?

2. Do people send greeting cards only on special occasions in your country? Compare the tradition of sending cards in the United States and in your country.

3. Hallmark makes cards for over 100 family relationships. How many different relationships are there in your family?

Part One

What a Doll!

Before You Read

1. Discuss In small groups, discuss the following questions: What was your favorite toy or doll when you were a child? What are the most popular toys and dolls in your country today?

While You Read

2. Match Drawings and Paragraphs Match each paragraph of the reading on page 11 with one of the pictures below. Compare answers with a partner.

1. _____

2. _____

3. _D_

4. _____

Barbie® is a registered trademark of Mattel, Inc.

Barbie: What a Doll!

A   She's now middle-aged, but she still has long hair, a great figure, and fashionable clothes. She has a popular sister named Skipper, and a good-looking boyfriend named Ken. Her circle of friends includes Midge, her best friend, and Becky, a new friend who is disabled.

B   She's just a doll, and she's called Barbie. Mattel, a toy manufacturer, introduced the Barbie doll in 1959. The company described her as "a shapely teenage fashion model." Since then, the Barbie doll has had many careers, including doctor, astronaut, and paleontologist. Mattel has produced nearly a billion dolls representing different races and ethnic groups. The Barbie doll, only 11½ inches high, has become the most successful doll in history.

C   Clearly, many little girls love to play with and collect Barbie dolls. Adults are collectors, too. But some parents are not happy with the Barbie doll. They think the doll represents a limited and unrealistic standard of beauty. Another problem is cost. While the average Barbie doll is not very expensive, a typical girl in the United States owns eight of them.

D   But loved or not, the Barbie doll continues to be popular. She has been the focus of a movie, a painting by the artist Andy Warhol, and many photography exhibits. There are books about her, and a museum in Palo Alto, California, is devoted to her. The Barbie doll is a part of Americana.

After You Read

3. React to the Reading   On a separate sheet of paper, write your reaction to something that surprised or interested you in the reading. Then, in small groups, share your reactions.

4. Say Why   Why are some parents not happy with the Barbie doll? Write your answer based on the reading, then write what *you* think. Discuss your answers in small groups.

According to the reading: _____

_____

In my opinion: _____

_____

5. Look for Evidence   The examples that support a statement are called evidence. Use evidence from the reading to answer the following questions. Compare answers with a partner.

1.   What evidence shows that the Barbie doll has become part of Americana?

_____

2.   What evidence shows that the Barbie doll is successful?

_____

6. Match Drawings and Statements   Match each sentence based on the reading with one of the drawings below. Compare answers with a partner.

a. She's a shapely teenage fashion model.
b. I have my own museum.
c. It's an unrealistic standard of beauty.
d. Please buy me another Barbie doll.

1. _____

2. _____

3. _____

4. _____

7. Understand the Words   Match each word or phrase in the left column with the correct meaning on the right.

WORDS

_____ **1.** She's now <u>middle-aged</u>.

_C_ **2.** The Becky doll is <u>disabled</u>.

_____ **3.** Adults are <u>collectors</u> too.

_____ **4.** She is <u>a part of Americana</u>.

_____ **5.** It's <u>a limited standard</u> of beauty.

MEANING

a. something typical of the United States

b. between 40 and 60 years old

c. physically or mentally disadvantaged

d. only one type or model

e. people who acquire items as a hobby

8. Write Sentences   On a separate sheet of paper, write a new sentence with each underlined word or phrase from Exercise 7. Work with a partner, and take turns writing the sentences.

9. Put Sentences in Order   Work with a partner. Number the following
sentences in the correct order from 1 to 5. Then close your book and try to tell
your partner the sentences in order.

_____ Since then, the Barbie doll has had many careers, and Mattel has produced almost a billion
dolls.

__1__ The Barbie doll is getting older, but she looks the same.

_____ But some parents don't like the doll.

_____ When Mattel introduced the Barbie doll in 1959, the company described her as a teenage
fashion model.

_____ Loved or not, the Barbie doll has become a part of Americana.

10. Complete the Categories   Work with a partner. Use words from the
reading, as well as your own examples, to complete each category. Compare
answers with other students. Who has the most examples?

THE ARTS	CAREERS	PEOPLE
1. _____	2. _____	3. ___sister___
_____	_____	_____
_____	_____	_____
_____	_____	_____
_____	_____	_____
_____	_____	_____
_____	_____	_____
_____	_____	_____
_____	_____	_____

11. Write and Discuss   On a separate sheet of paper, write your answers to the
following questions. Then discuss your opinions in small groups.

1. What's your reaction to America's love of the Barbie doll?
2. Many Americans are fascinated by top fashion models, called supermodels. Is the Barbie doll just
another example of this fascination?
3. What kind of toys will you (or do you) buy for your children? Why?

Part Two

Talking Dolls

Before You Read

1. Discuss the Solution   In small groups, discuss the following question: What should parents do if they think a popular toy is bad for their child? Some possibilities are given below. Share your group's opinions with the class.

- Buy the toy, but tell the child why it's bad.
- Don't buy the toy and tell the child why it's bad.
- Write a letter to the manufacturer asking the company to stop making the toy.
- Write a letter to a newspaper explaining why the toy is bad.

- (Your suggestion) _____

_____

_____

2. Look for the Point of View   In the drawing above, what is the mother's point of view, or opinion, of some children's toys? Discuss this question with a partner. Then share your answers in small groups.

While You Read

3. Look for Evidence   Think about the point of view of the group of artists and parents in the reading on page 15. What evidence supports this point of view? Write your ideas below.

Evidence: _____

_____

_____

_____

A   One recent December, many parents went shopping for dolls for their children—Barbie dolls for girls and G.I. Joe dolls for boys. Talking versions of the dolls were popular that year. But some children were going to get a big surprise.

B   A group of artists and parents in New York City had bought 300 talking Barbie and G.I. Joe dolls and switched their voice boxes. Then they returned the dolls to the toy stores to be sold again.

C   When a little boy opened his altered G.I. Joe doll and pushed the talk button, he got a surprise. The boy doll sweetly said, "Let's go shopping!" and "Let's plan our dream wedding!" When a girl opened her altered Barbie doll, the doll said in a deep voice, "Attack! Eat lead, Cobra!"

D   A letter from the group came in the box with each doll. It explained that toys like the G.I. Joe doll can teach boys to be violent, and toys like the Barbie doll can teach girls to focus too much on clothes and weddings. The message was that these male and female stereotypes were bad for kids.

E   The letter asked parents to tell their stories to the news media. The news of the sweet-talking G.I. Joe and tough-talking Barbie dolls spread the group's message across the country.

After You Read

4. React to the Reading   On a separate sheet of paper, write your reaction to something that surprised or interested you in the reading. Then, in small groups, share your reactions.

5. Read in Groups of Words   Read the example below. Then, as you listen to your instructor read "Talking Dolls" in groups of words, circle each group you hear. Remember that you can read faster and understand more if you read in groups of words.

EXAMPLE: (One recent December,)   (many parents went shopping for dolls)
(for their children) — (Barbie dolls for girls)   (and G.I. Joe dolls for boys.)

When you finish, read it again silently in groups of words.

6. Match Topics and Paragraphs   Match each of the following topics with a paragraph from the reading. Write the letters of the paragraphs on the lines. Compare answers with a partner.

_____ **1.** what the group's message was

__A__ **2.** what parents were buying for their children that December

_____ **3.** what the altered dolls said

_____ **4.** what a group of artists and parents did to the dolls

_____ **5.** what the group wanted the parents to do

7. Pick the Summary   Read the following summaries. Then check the one that best summarizes the reading. Compare answers with a partner.

☐ **1.** Sweet-talking G.I. Joe dolls and tough-talking Barbie dolls surprised many children.

☐ **2.** One recent December, some boys opened their presents and found G.I. Joe dolls that said, "Let's go shopping!"

☐ **3.** A New York City group switched the Barbie doll's and the G.I. Joe doll's voice boxes to spread a message about stereotypes.

8. Look for the Point of View   Read the following personal opinions and think about each speaker's point of view. Then check whether the speaker is *for* or *against* the Barbie doll. Compare answers with a partner.

1. "I know what you're going to say. The Barbie doll represents the dumb blond: clothes, dates, and her wedding are all she thinks about. But maybe some little girls like to think about those things. What's wrong with that?"

This parent is   ☐ for the Barbie doll   ☐ against the Barbie doll

2. "In 1992 Mattel put out a version of the Barbie doll that said, "Math class is hard." Fortunately, a lot of people complained, and the company stopped making it. But the Barbie doll is still talking about clothes and shopping. What kind of model is that for little girls?"

This parent is   ☐ for the Barbie doll   ☐ against the Barbie doll

9. React to the Point of View   On a separate sheet of paper, write your reaction to one of the points of view in Exercise 8. Do you agree or disagree with the speaker's point of view? Why? Then, in small groups, share your reactions.

10. Complete the Conversation Use words from the box to complete the conversation. Compare answers with a partner.

altered	✓dolls	parent
children	message	stereotypes

TINA: Did you know there are _____dolls_____ [1] today that carry a social _____ [2]?

YOKO: What do you mean—like "Just say no"?*

TINA: No, they're _____ [3] dolls. They're not the traditional _____ [4] of women.

YOKO: I don't follow.

TINA: Well, there's the Divorced doll, the Teenage Single Parent doll, and . . .

YOKO: Wait a second! What _____ [5] would buy dolls like that for their _____ [6]?

TINA: They're not for kids; they're for adults!

*A slogan used in the United States to help young people say no to drugs.

11. Write and Discuss Read **Just the Facts.** Then read the questions that follow and write your answers on a separate sheet of paper. Discuss your answers in small groups.

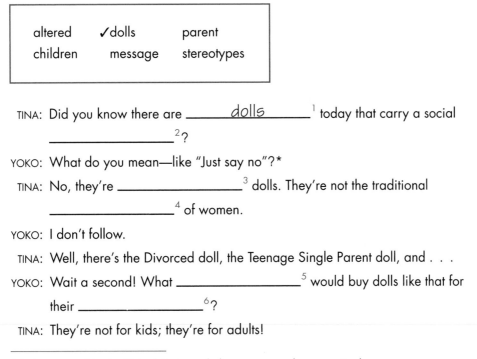

Just the Facts: Barbie Dolls

- Barbie dolls are sold in 140 countries.
- Around the world, two Barbie dolls are sold every second.
- In 1959, a Barbie doll cost $3. Today, a Barbie doll from 1959 can cost $3,000 to $5,000.
- The Barbie doll museum in California has more than 16,000 Barbie dolls.
- The best-selling Barbie doll was Totally Hair Barbie, who had hair down to her feet.

1. What do you think of the Barbie doll as an American export?
2. If the doll is a female stereotype, why is she still popular today?
3. Should the Barbie doll be blamed for the eating disorders—such as too much dieting to stay thin—that many young women have today? Why or why not?

Part One

The American Folk Hero

Before You Read

1. Match Words and Drawings Work with a partner. Match each item below with the appropriate drawing.

branding iron
cattle drive
✓ lasso
riding a bronco
roping a calf
stagecoach robbery

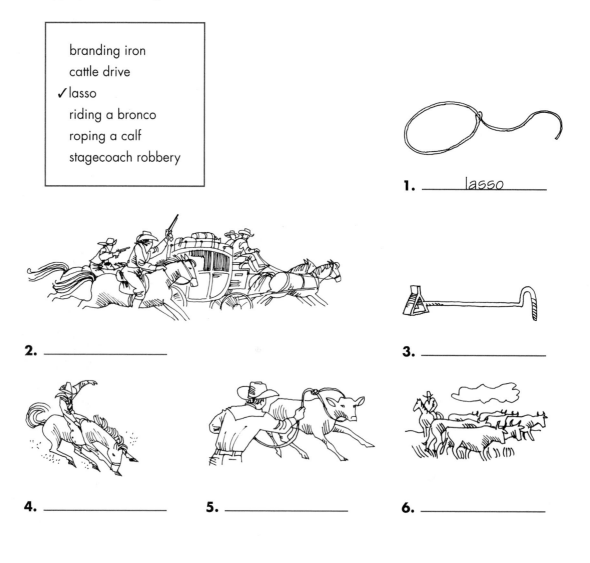

1. _____lasso_____

2. _____

3. _____

4. _____

5. _____

6. _____

While You Read

2. Mark the Text While you read "The American Folk Hero," underline the following information:

a. what the cowboy symbolizes
b. how news of the cowboy spread across the country

Then compare answers with a partner.

The American Folk Hero

A   To many, the cowboy is a symbol of freedom and adventure. He rides a horse across vast, open country from sunup to sundown. At night, he sleeps under the stars.

B   Cowboys lived on the Great Plains, starting in the nineteenth century. About 75 percent of them were white, but about 25 percent were African American, Native American, and Mexican American. Cowboys, as the name suggests, took care of cows and other cattle. They helped with births and protected the cattle from thieves and wild animals. They also drove the cattle to railroad towns to be sold. Their tools were a branding iron, a lasso, and a gun.

C   At the end of a long cattle drive, cowboys were paid for their work. With plenty of money in their pockets, they often went wild in cattle towns, such as Dodge City, Kansas, or Cheyenne, Wyoming. They drank, sang songs, played cards, and fought in the streets and bars. But cowboys also got together to show off their skills. These gatherings developed into rodeos. The most famous rodeo was Buffalo Bill's Wild West. In it, cowboys acted out stagecoach robberies and battles with Indians. They demonstrated how to rope a calf and ride a bronco. Cowgirls like Annie Oakley displayed their shooting skills. Sitting Bull and other Native Americans acted out Indian ceremonies.

D   By the 1860s, dime novels—inexpensive paperback books about the West—were spreading the legend of the cowboy. In 1902, one of these novels, *The Virginian,* was published. It told the tale of a cowboy in the West and the woman he loved, a schoolteacher from the East. It also described the harsh rules the cowboy lived by: "Might makes right" and "Kill or be killed." This best-selling novel and the play, movies, and television shows based on it helped make the cowboy *the* American folk hero.

After You Read

3. Read in Groups of Words   Read the example below. Then, as you listen to your instructor read "The American Folk Hero" in groups of words, circle each group you hear. Remember that you can read faster and understand more if you read in groups of words.

EXAMPLE: (To many,)   (the cowboy)   (is a symbol of freedom and adventure.)

(He rides a horse)   (across vast,)   (open country)

(from sunup to sundown.)

When you finish, read it again silently in groups of words.

4. Match Topics and Paragraphs   Match each of the following topics with a paragraph from the reading. Write the letters of the paragraphs on the lines. Compare answers with a partner.

_____ **1.** who cowboys were and what they did

_____ **2.** how the legend of the cowboy spread

_____ **3.** what the cowboy represents to many Americans

_____ **4.** what cowboys did after a cattle drive, and how rodeos developed

5. Pick the Summary   Read the following summaries. Then check the one that best summarizes the reading. Compare answers with a partner.

☐ **1.** Most cowboys were white, but some were African American, Native American, and Mexican American.

☐ **2.** Buffalo Bill's Wild West, the most famous rodeo, included stagecoach robberies, battles with Indians, calf roping, bronco riding, sharp shooting, and Indian ceremonies.

☐ **3.** Originally, cowboys took care of cattle on the Great Plains. They also drove cattle to railroad towns and started the first rodeos. Later, books, plays, movies, and television made them American folk heroes.

6. Complete the Conversation
Use words from the box to complete the conversation. Compare answers with a partner.

adventure
✓cattle drive
got together
lasso
ride
went wild

MAX: Look at this story in the paper. More than fifty people _____[1]

for a ___cattle drive___[2], just like real cowboys. They followed part of

the old Chisholm Trail, from Texas north through Oklahoma.

RICK: That's quite an _____[3]! How many cattle did they move?

MAX: Three hundred.

RICK: I wonder how many of those urban cowboys knew how to

_____[4] a horse and use a _____.[5]

MAX: It doesn't say. You know, in the old days, the cowboys

_____[6] at the end of a cattle drive. They drank in bars, spent

their money, and then had to ride back to Texas.

RICK: Wow! I bet those modern cowboys just climbed into an airplane and flew

home!

7. Write and Discuss
Write your answers to the following questions on a separate sheet of paper. Then discuss your opinions in small groups.

1. Why do you think people in the United States like the legend of the cowboy so much?
2. Is the cowboy "a symbol of freedom and adventure" to you? If not, what does the cowboy represent to you?
3. Who is the most popular folk hero in your country? Is it a prince, a worker, a soldier, a sailor, or someone else? How is this hero different from the cowboy?

Part Two

The Cowboy Legend Lives On

Before You Read

1. Predict   Look at the pictures below in Exercise 2. Working with a partner, predict what the next reading will be about. Write your predictions here:

_____

_____

_____

While You Read

2. Match Pictures and Paragraphs   Match each paragraph from the reading on page 23 with one of the pictures below. Compare answers with a partner.

1. _D_

2. ___

3. ___

4. ___

A   Today, the cowboy continues to have a place in American popular culture. Although the number of working cowboys is getting smaller, the legend of the cowboy is kept alive in books, movies, and television shows. It is also preserved in a growing number of rodeos and museums.

B   Just as the nineteenth-century cowboy rode his horse across the prairie, today's rodeo cowboy drives his truck across the western highways from one rodeo to the next. Some spend as many as 200 days a year on the road. In the competitions, they show off the cowboy skills that many of them learned in colleges of the West.

C   In the 1990s, the number of professional rodeos in the United States increased 25 percent to over 800 a year. Americans now watch young men, and a few women, rope calves, wrestle steers, and ride broncos in competition for prize money. For the spectators, these rodeos provide a live connection to the rugged, romantic American past.

D   Another way locals and visitors to the West can experience the American past is through cowboy museums. These museums show the excitement of nineteenth-century life on the plains, and some also tell the stories of twentieth-century movie and television cowboys such as Gene Autry, John Wayne, and the famous western couple, Roy Rogers and Dale Evans. Some of the museums display paintings by Charles M. Russell, and sculptures of cowboys and Native Americans by Frederic Remington. Village museums, also called living museums, recreate entire communities of the old West. Here visitors can walk through the streets or ride in a stagecoach and watch actors play the roles of cowboys and townspeople baking bread, making soap, and shoeing horses. This allows the visitors to return in their imagination to the simpler, freer, and more exciting times of the cowboy.

After You Read

3. Check Your Predictions   Go back to Exercise 1 to see if your predictions were correct. Discuss them with a partner and make changes, if necessary.

4. Pick a Title   Work with a partner. Pick another title for the reading. Check one of the following boxes. The title gives the subject of the reading.

☐ **1.** Competing for Prize Money in Rodeos

☐ **2.** Cowboy Museums

☐ **3.** Rodeos and Museums Keep the Legend of the Cowboy Alive

Discuss why the other two are not good titles.

5. Put Sentences in Order   Work with a partner. Number the following
sentences in the correct order from 1 to 6. Then close your book and try to tell
your partner the sentences in order.

_____ By watching these rodeo cowboys rope calves, wrestle steers, and ride broncos, Americans
become connected to the country's past.

_____ These museums tell the stories of both authentic and television cowboys and cowgirls.

__1__ Today, rodeos and museums help keep the legend of the cowboy alive.

_____ Living museums help the visitor experience the exciting life and times of the cowboy.

_____ Cowboy museums are another way of experiencing America's past.

_____ At rodeos, cowboys show off skills many of them learned in college.

6. Say Where to Go   For each situation below, recommend either a rodeo,
cowboy museum, or village museum. Write your answers on the lines below. Then
compare answers with a partner.

TO SEE . . .	GO TO A . . .
1. a sculpture by Frederic Remington	_____
2. a real cowboy ride a bronco	_____
3. television cowboys and cowgirls	_____
4. the streets and towns of the old West	_____
5. cowboys compete for prize money	_____
6. a stagecoach ride	_____

7. Pick the Summary   Read the following summaries. Then check the one that
best summarizes the reading. Compare answers with a partner.

☐ **1.** Today, while there are fewer working cowboys than in the past, the legend of the cowboy is
preserved in rodeos and cowboy museums.

☐ **2.** The legend of the cowboy is preserved in books, movies, and television shows.

☐ **3.** In village museums, visitors can walk through the streets or take a stagecoach ride and watch
actors play the roles of cowboys and townspeople.

8. Complete the Conversation Use words from the box to complete the conversation. Compare answers with a partner.

cowboy
on the road
✓prairie
rodeo
simpler
living

TINA: I've always wanted to drive across country, visit the West, and travel across
the _____prairie_____.[1]

YOKO: Are you crazy? Do you know how far it is? You'll be
_____[2] for weeks.

TINA: So what? I want to experience a different way of life. I'll camp out, watch a
_____[3], see some cowboys, and visit those
_____[4] museums.

YOKO: Wait a second. What you're saying is you want to be a tourist out West.

TINA: No, maybe I'll move out there. Life sounds _____[5] there.
Maybe I'll become a cowgirl and rope myself a _____.[6]

YOKO: Now I get it!

9. Write and Discuss Read **Just the Facts**. Then read the questions that follow and write your answers on a separate sheet of paper. Discuss your answers in small groups.

Just the Facts: Cowboys and Cattle

- Columbus brought the first cattle to the New World on his second voyage in 1493.
- Some cattle drives were 1,500 miles (nearly 2,500 kilometers) long.
- By 1890, guns were illegal in most western towns, but people didn't always follow the law.
- The largest cowboy museum is the Buffalo Bill Historical Center in Cody, Wyoming.

1.   Would you like to go on a cattle drive? Why or why not?
2.   Is the cowboy a popular image in your country? If yes, why do people like the cowboy?
3.   What is the image of the cowboy in novels and movies today? Is he still fearless and quick with a gun? Does he represent good or evil?

Unit One

Check Your Progress

You have just completed the first three chapters in this book. Take a minute to think about some of the things you have learned. Check all of the following statements that are true for you.

☐   I can understand the reading more when I look at the pictures.

☐   I can understand the reading even if I don't know every word.

☐   I can understand the reading more when I discuss it.

☐   I can learn from my partner and my group.

☐   I can learn the meaning of new words and expressions when I read.

Follow-Up

You can learn more about the topics in this unit by doing research and reporting your research to your class. You can also read books and watch movies about these topics. Here are some suggestions for each chapter.

Chapter 1

Research and Report. Go to a card shop and make a list of the different types of greeting cards sold there. Ask the sales clerk what the most popular cards are. Report the results to your class.

Chapter 2

Research and Report. Survey three families you know. What kinds of toys do they buy for their children? Do they buy different kinds of toys for boys and girls? Report the results to the class.

Chapter 3

Movies. Watch one of these movies in class or at home. Discuss your reactions.

City Slickers, a 1991 comedy, starring Billy Crystal (114 minutes)

High Noon, a 1952 classic, starring Gary Cooper (85 minutes)

Red River, a 1948 classic, starring John Wayne and Montgomery Clift (125 minutes)

Books. The following books are about the West.

Lonesome Dove, a novel by Larry McMurtry

All the Pretty Horses, a novel by Cormac McCarthy

The Cowgirl Companion, a history of women in the West by Gail Gilchriest

Symbols

Did You Know . . . ?
- Most people in the United States oppose flag burning.
- There has been a debate over a new presidential memorial in Washington, D.C.
- Uncle Sam is named after a meat merchant in New York.

In Unit Two, you will read about some symbols of the United States and where they came from. You will also learn how these symbols are used today in art and politics.

CHAPTER 4

Part One

The Stars and Stripes

Before You Read

1. Match Flags and Countries   The drawings show the flags of four countries. Work with a partner. Try to match the flags and the countries by writing the name of the country under each flag. Which flag do you like the best? Why?

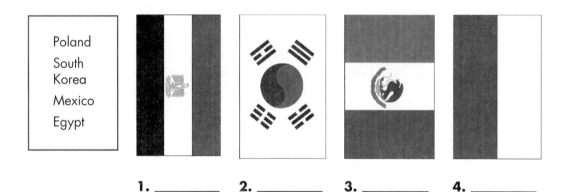

Poland
South Korea
Mexico
Egypt

1. _____   2. _____   3. _____   4. _____

While You Read

2. Match Pictures and Paragraphs   Match each paragraph of the reading on page 29 with one of the flags below. (One paragraph corresponds to two flags.) Compare answers with a partner.

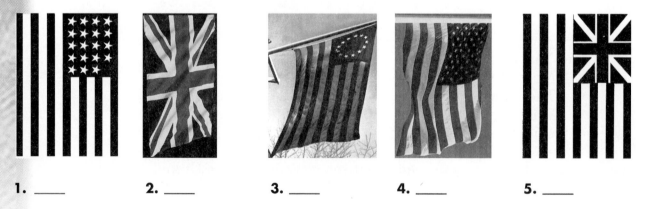

1. ____   2. ____   3. ____   4. ____   5. ____

A   The first flag of the thirteen colonies in America was the British flag called the Union Jack. At the beginning of the Revolutionary War (1775-1783), when the American colonies fought Great Britain for their independence, the colonial army carried a new flag. This flag, called the Grand Union flag, had the Union Jack in the upper-left corner. It also had thirteen red and white stripes to represent the thirteen colonies.

B   Shortly before the American colonies declared their independence from Great Britain on July 4, 1776, the leaders decided they needed a new flag. According to legend, General George Washington and members of Congress (the new American government) asked a Philadelphia dressmaker to design a flag for the new country. The dressmaker, Betsy Ross, used the same colors as the British flag—red, white, and blue—and the same thirteen stripes as the Grand Union flag. But in place of the Union Jack, she sewed thirteen white stars on a blue background. Each star and stripe represented one of the thirteen original states* in the United States of America. This flag was adopted by Congress on June 14, 1777.

C   As the United States grew and new states joined, more stars and stripes were added to the flag. With twenty states by 1818, it was not easy to add both stars and stripes to the flag. At that point, Congress voted to return to thirteen stripes to symbolize the thirteen original states and to add one star to symbolize each state.

D   After Alaska and Hawaii joined the United States in 1959, the number of states totaled fifty. Since then, the flag has consisted of fifty stars and thirteen stripes. Through 200 years of change, Betsy Ross's design has endured. Today, the Stars and Stripes is displayed each year outside homes on June 14, Flag Day.

*The states officially became part of the United States between 1787 and 1790.

After You Read

3. Pick a Title   Work with a partner. Pick another title for the reading. Check one of the following boxes. The title gives the subject of the reading.

☐ **1.** The Changing but Lasting United States Flag

☐ **2.** The Flag of the Thirteen Colonies

☐ **3.** Flag Day

Discuss why the other two are not good titles.

4. Read in Groups of Words   You now know that you can read faster and understand more if you read in groups of words. But which words go together in a group? Here are some tips:

noun phrase:	The first flag of the thirteen colonies in America
verb phrase:	was the British flag called the Union Jack.
prepositional phrase:	At the beginning of the Revolutionary War,
clause:	when the American colonies fought Great Britain for their independence,
words inside parentheses:	(the new American government)
words inside dashes:	—red, white, and blue—
words inside a comma and a period:	, Flag Day.

Work with a partner. Use these tips to circle each group of words in the reading on page 29. Then, as your instructor reads in groups of words, check what you circled. When you finish, read it again silently in groups of words.

5. Put Sentences in Order   Work with a partner. Number the following sentences in the correct order from 1 to 6. Then close your book and try to tell your partner the sentences in order.

_____ More stars and stripes were added as more states joined the country.

_____ Betsy Ross's basic design has lasted over 200 years.

_____ When the colonies fought the British in the Revolutionary War, the Grand Union flag replaced the Union Jack.

_____ When there were twenty states, Congress decided to limit the stripes to thirteen and have one star represent each state.

__1__ Originally, the British flag represented the thirteen colonies in America.

_____ Betsy Ross designed a flag with stars and stripes for the newly independent United States of America.

6. Make Statements   Use information from the reading on page 29 to make statements about the number of states in the United States and the country's growth. Compare answers with a partner.

1. In the late 1700s, the country _____

2. By 1818, _____

3. Between 1818 and 1959, _____

4. From 1959 to today, _____

7. Complete the Conversation   Use words from the box to complete the conversation. Compare answers with partner.

Day
✓displayed
flag
symbolize

YOKO: Why are so many flags being ___displayed___ [1] today?

TINA: It's Flag _____.[2]

YOKO: Why do you think national flags are such a big deal?

TINA: They _____[3] each country.

YOKO: But, for example, in the United States, how can a piece of cloth represent 260 million people?

TINA: Would you rather have one flag for each person?

YOKO: Actually, that's not a bad idea—my own personal _____.[4]

8. Direct and Draw   Draw a flag you know well (or use one of the flags on page 28). Don't show it to your partner. Give your partner directions for drawing it by using some of the words below. Then compare drawings with your partner. Do they match? If not, what went wrong? Then switch roles so that your partner gives you directions.

in the upper-left corner	in the center	stars	square
in the lower-left corner	in the background	stripes	rectangle
in the upper-right corner	draw	lines	triangle
in the lower-right corner	add	circle	

Listening Strategy

If you can't follow the directions, you can say:
"Sorry, I couldn't follow that." (Your partner should give you the directions again.)

---

9. Write and Discuss   On a separate sheet of paper, write your answers to the following questions. Then discuss your opinions in small groups.

1. What does the United States flag symbolize to people in your country?
2. Do you think it's too patriotic to display a flag outside your home? Why?
3. Do you think Puerto Rico will become the fifty-first state someday? What are the arguments for or against this proposal?

The Flag: From Painting to Politics

Before You Read

1. Take a Quiz   What do you already know about the United States flag? Work with a partner. Complete the following sentences by circling the letter of each correct answer.

---

1. The U.S. flag is called
   a. the Stars and Stripes
   b. Old Glory
   c. the Star-Spangled Banner
   d. all of the above
2. Flag-burning for political reasons is
   a. legal
   b. illegal

3. Flag Day in the U.S. is
   a. July 4th
   b. June 14th
   c. January 1st

While You Read

2. Match Pictures and Paragraphs   Match three paragraphs from the reading on page 33 with the three pictures below. Then write the letters of the three other paragraphs that have no matching picture: _____, _____, and _____.

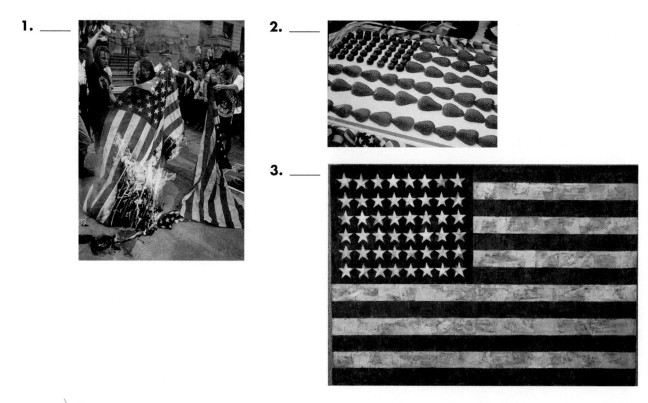

1. _____

2. _____

3. _____

A   A country's flag is its most common symbol. A symbol, however, can mean different things to different people. To some Americans, the Stars and Stripes is a symbol of patriotism—a feeling of love, respect, and sacrifice for one's country. To others, it's a symbol of freedom. That freedom includes the right to use the flag for everything from painting to politics.

B   To veterans, the flag is a symbol of the courage and patriotism of those who fought in wars and died for their country. Other groups display the flag to show their support for traditional values. These groups want the flag to be treated with respect. They like to see the flag in front of government buildings and outside homes on Flag Day and other national holidays.

C   The Stars and Stripes has also inspired many works of art. The artist Jasper Johns has painted the flag several times. One of his works is simply called *Flag*. It has only forty-eight stars because it was painted before Alaska and Hawaii became part of the United States.

D   Fashion designers, too, have used the flag in their work. They have created flag shirts, flag ties, flag jackets, flag shoes, and even flag bikinis. In the liberal 1960s and 1970s, some young people wore jeans with a flag on the seat of the pants to protest patriotism. In the more conservative 1980s and 1990s, flag fashions were a symbol of patriotism.

E   Bakers have also found inspiration in the Stars and Stripes. Every summer, just before the Fourth of July, many bakeries sell cakes in the form of the flag. The stars are blueberries on a background of whipped cream. The stripes are lines of strawberries and whipped cream.

F   Political groups have often used the flag as a symbol. Many groups have burned the flag to protest government policies. Flag burning makes many Americans angry. In fact, forty-eight states have passed laws against it. However, in 1989, the Supreme Court decided that it *is* legal to burn the flag during a political demonstration. The Court decided that flag burning is a form of free speech which is protected by the Constitution.

After You Read

3. React to the Reading   On a separate sheet of paper, write your reaction to something that surprised you in the reading. Then, in small groups, share your reactions.

4. Look for Examples   Good writing often includes examples to support the main ideas. Read the following main ideas. Then find at least one example in the reading to support each idea. Compare answers with a partner.

1.   The flag represents different things to different Americans:

_____

_____

_____

2.   The flag has inspired art, fashion, and food:

_____

_____

_____

3.   The flag is used for political purposes:

_____

_____

_____

5. Mark the Summary   Scan the reading and find the sentence (or sentences) that summarizes the reading. Write it on the lines below. Compare answers with a partner.

_____

_____

6. Complete the Categories   Work with a partner. Use words from the reading, as well as your own, to complete each category. Compare lists with other students. Who has the most words?

CLOTHES	STATES	OCCUPATIONS	OTHER GROUPS
1. _____	2. _____	3. _____	4. _____
_____	_____	_____	_____
_____	_____	_____	_____
_____	_____	_____	_____
_____	_____	_____	_____

7. Complete the Conversation Use words from the box to complete the conversation. Compare answers with a partner.

died
flag
fought
Patriotism
✓shirt
wear

MAX: Why would anyone want to wear a bicycle _____shirt_____[1] with a flag on it?

RICK: _____.[2] Remember what Alexis de Tocqueville said: "Americans are the most patriotic people on earth."

MAX: But do they have to _____[3] their flag? Some people even become emotional about flags. I don't get it.

RICK: Maybe they had family members who fought in wars and _____[4] for their country.

MAX: What if no one ever _____[5] in wars?

RICK: We'd still be part of England and have a different _____.[6]

8. Write and Discuss Read **Just the Facts**. Then read the questions that follow and write answers to them on a separate sheet of paper. Discuss your answers in small groups.

Just the Facts: The U.S. Flag

- The largest American flag flew from the Verrazano Narrows Bridge in New York City on Independence Day (July 4), 1982. It was bigger than a football field and cost a million dollars.
- Between 1980 and 1989, there was a 90 percent increase in the sale of American flags.*
- In a survey in 1989, 71 percent of Americans said they wanted flag burning to be illegal.[†]

Source: *Harper's Index; [†]The Newsweek Poll © 1989 by Newsweek, Inc.

1. What is your opinion of flag burning? Should it be legal or illegal? Why?
2. In the last twenty years, do you think your country has become more or less patriotic? What evidence supports this?
3. Do you think Americans are more patriotic than people in other countries? Why or why not?

Part One

The White House

Before You Read

1. Discuss In small groups, discuss the following question: Should the president or head of a country live in a palace like a king or queen, or in a small, simple house? Why?

While You Read

2. Match Pictures and Paragraphs Match four of the five paragraphs from the reading on page 37 with the pictures below. Compare answers with a partner.

1. _____

2. __C__

3. _____

4. _____

A   The big, white house at 1600 Pennsylvania Avenue is not an ordinary house. It's the official home of the president. Every president has lived there, except one. George Washington was president (1789-1797) before work on this house was completed.

B   In the early 1800s, people called the building the presidential palace or the executive mansion. It's a three-story structure made of limestone, a white-gray stone. It originally had one hundred rooms. Over the years, thirty-two rooms have been added. One of these is the famous Oval Office where the president works.

C   The architect of the White House was an Irish immigrant named James Hoban. In 1792, Hoban won a contest for the best design for the president's house.

D   Work began in 1792 and was completed in 1800. At that point, the second president, John Adams, moved in. But during the War of 1812, the British army burned the city of Washington, D.C. In 1814, the executive mansion was destroyed in a fire. Dolley Madison, the wife of President James Madison, saved a painting of George Washington and many important documents from the fire. After the war, the presidential home was rebuilt, enlarged, and painted white. Soon, people in Washington, D.C. began to call it the White House because it was the only white house in a neighborhood of red brick buildings. That name became official in 1902.

E   Another white house in another country looks very much like the one in Washington, D.C. People usually think this house is a copy of the White House, but it's actually the other way around. This one, called Leinster House, is in Dublin, Ireland. It's the home of the Irish parliament. It was built almost fifty years earlier and was the model for Hoban's design.

After You Read

3. Look for the Main Idea   What does the last paragraph of the reading tell you about the White House? Write the main idea of the last paragraph on the lines below. Compare answers with a partner.

_____

_____

_____

4. Look for Details   What happened to the White House? Look at the time line below and on the next page. Then scan the reading for the missing information and write it on the lines provided. Compare answers with a partner.

			The White House was rebuilt.	The North Portico was built.
1792	1800	1814	1815–1817	1824

5. Complete the Letter   Use words from the box to complete the letter.

official
painting
President
rooms
works

Dear Natasha,

   I'm looking forward to your visit to D.C. I've been checking into things we could do. I visited the White House Friday and took the _____¹ tour. Although the building has 132 _____,² they showed us only seven. It was interesting to see how the _____³ and First Lady live. Of course, we didn't see the Oval Office, where the President _____,⁴ but we did visit the East Room with the famous _____⁵ of George Washington by Gilbert Stuart. (The presidential look has changed!) We also visited the Lincoln bedroom. Rich people sometimes get to sleep here—for a price. I think you'd prefer a hotel.

                                        Love, Max

The South Portico was added.	_____ _____ _____	President Taft enlarged the West Wing to create the Oval Office.	Forty-two layers of paint were removed and the house was repainted.
1829	1902	1909	1980–1992

6. Ask for the Meaning   Choose three new words from the reading on page 37 and write them below. Work in small groups. Ask other students if they know the meaning of each word. Write the meaning on the lines provided. If necessary, look up the meaning in a dictionary.

> ## Speaking Strategy
>
> To ask for the meaning of a word, you can say: "Do you know what *contest* means?"

	WORDS		MEANING
1.	_____	=	_____
2.	_____	=	_____
3.	_____	=	_____

7. Write and Discuss   On a separate sheet of paper, write your answers to the following questions. Then discuss your opinions in small groups.

1. Where does the leader of your country live? What do you think of your leader's house?
2. The American poet Walt Whitman (1819–1892) wrote: "A great city is that which has the greatest men and women." Do you agree? Is Washington, D.C. a great city according to Whitman's definition?

The FDR Memorial

Before You Read

1. Interview First, write your own answers to the following survey questions. Then interview your partner and write his or her answers. Discuss your answers with your partner.

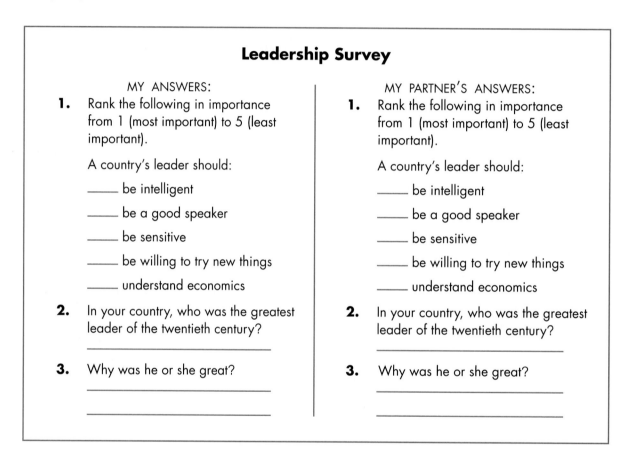

Leadership Survey

MY ANSWERS:

1. Rank the following in importance from 1 (most important) to 5 (least important).

    A country's leader should:

    _____ be intelligent

    _____ be a good speaker

    _____ be sensitive

    _____ be willing to try new things

    _____ understand economics

2. In your country, who was the greatest leader of the twentieth century?

    _____

3. Why was he or she great?

    _____

    _____

MY PARTNER'S ANSWERS:

1. Rank the following in importance from 1 (most important) to 5 (least important).

    A country's leader should:

    _____ be intelligent

    _____ be a good speaker

    _____ be sensitive

    _____ be willing to try new things

    _____ understand economics

2. In your country, who was the greatest leader of the twentieth century?

    _____

3. Why was he or she great?

    _____

    _____

While You Read

2. Describe a Drawing for Each Paragraph Think about a drawing that would illustrate the most important idea in each paragraph of the reading on page 41. Describe each drawing below. Then compare answers with a partner.

Paragraph A: _____

Paragraph B: _____

Paragraph C: _____

Paragraph D: _____

A   Washington, D.C., the nation's capital, is famous for its buildings and monuments. Some of the most popular are the White House and the memorials to the nation's greatest presidents: Washington, Jefferson, and Lincoln.

B   In 1997, a new monument opened in Washington. It is in memory of the president many Americans believe to be the twentieth century's greatest, Franklin Delano Roosevelt. Known as FDR, he provided strong leadership during the depression and World War II. But the monument, like FDR's presidency, has not been without controversy.

C   When Roosevelt was first elected president, the country was in the middle of the economic crisis known as the Great Depression (1929–1939). FDR called for a New Deal for the American people. The idea was for the government to borrow money to pay people to work. The government hired many people to build schools and roads, plant trees, and create parks. These new jobs did not bring back economic prosperity, but they did bring hope to millions of people. The people repaid FDR's faith in them by reelecting him president. He became the only president to serve four consecutive terms (1933–1945).

D   Why was the FDR Memorial so controversial? One problem was the high cost of the monument, 42.5 million dollars in federal funds (plus 5.5 million in private money). The second issue involved a sculpture of First Lady Eleanor Roosevelt wearing a fur. Animal rights groups complained, and the statue was changed. The third issue concerned FDR's disability. FDR was paralyzed at age 39 by the disease polio. For the rest of his life, he could not walk without help. He wore leg braces and used a wheelchair, but his disability was largely hidden from the American people. Many disabled Americans wanted a wheelchair to be part of the memorial. It would show that FDR was handicapped but overcame his disability. A fourth problem was that many people didn't like FDR's high levels of government spending. They did not want the monument to be a symbol of what were, in their view, bad government policies. And, finally, Roosevelt himself never wanted a memorial, just a simple plaque.

After You Read

3. React to the Reading   On a separate sheet of paper, write your reaction to something that surprised or interested you in the reading. Then, in small groups, share your reactions.

4. Correct the Summary   The following is a summary of the reading on the FDR Memorial. First, cross out the mistakes in each sentence. Then write your corrections above them.

Washington, D.C.

The most recent presidential monument in ~~New York~~ is the FDR Memorial.

Many Americans believe that Roosevelt was the greatest president of the

nineteenth century. FDR led the country through the economic crisis known

as the Bad Depression. His New Deal gave people in Europe jobs and

hope. When the FDR Memorial opened in 1997, everybody was happy.

5. Look for Examples   You now know that good writing often includes examples to support the main ideas. Read the following main ideas. Then find at least two examples in the reading to support each idea. Compare answers with a partner.

1.   Monuments to great presidents are popular in Washington, D.C:

_____

_____

_____

2.   During the Great Depression, the government gave people jobs:

_____

_____

_____

3.   The FDR Memorial was controversial:

_____

_____

_____

6. Match Pictures and Statements   Match each statement with one of the pictures below. Compare answers with a partner.

1. ____   **2.** ____   **3.** ____   **4.** ____

a. "I went to see the FDR Memorial this weekend. It's along the famous Cherry Tree Walk on the Tidal Basin."

b. "It's very different from the tall Washington Monument and the classical Jefferson and Lincoln Memorials."

c. "It has four outdoor rooms with sculptures, and quotations carved in the stone walls."

d. "You know, it's the first presidential memorial that honors a First Lady. Eleanor Roosevelt was a champion of the poor and the first U.S. delegate to the United Nations."

7. Write and Discuss   Read **Just the Facts**. Then read the questions that follow and write your answers on a separate sheet of paper. Discuss your answers in small groups.

Just the Facts: Presidents, First Ladies, the White House, and Presidential Monuments

- The president's salary is $200,000 a year plus $50,000 for expenses, and up to $100,000 for travel. The vice president's salary is $160,000 a year.
- Each year 1.2 million people tour the White House.
- Eleanor Roosevelt was the niece of President Theodore Roosevelt and a distant cousin of FDR.
- The San Francisco architect Lawrence Halprin won a competition for his design of the FDR Memorial in 1974. Construction began twenty years later.

1. Do you think the White House should be open to the public for tours? Why or why not?

2. Eleanor Roosevelt and Hillary Clinton played active roles in the White House. Do you think it's good for the president's spouse to play such an active role?

3. How do you feel about the following controversies over the FDR Memorial? Explain your opinions.

   a. the high cost   **d.** the memorial as a symbol of government spending

   b. Eleanor Roosevelt wearing a fur   **e.** FDR's wish for a plaque

   c. the lack of a wheelchair

Part One

Uncle Sam

Before You Read

1. Discuss In small groups, discuss the following question: What does the name *Uncle Sam* mean to you?

While You Read

2. Match Pictures and Paragraphs Match each paragraph of the reading on page 45 with one of the pictures below. Compare answers with a partner.

1. ____

2. ____

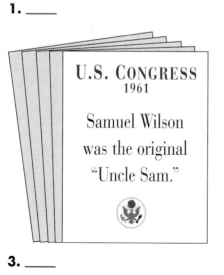

U.S. CONGRESS
1961

Samuel Wilson
was the original
"Uncle Sam."

3. ____

4. ____

A   Every citizen of the United States has an Uncle Sam. He has long white hair and whiskers. He wears a top hat, coat, vest, and striped pants. Who is this uncle?

B   To answer the question, it's necessary to go back to the War of 1812 (a war between the United States and Britain, which ended in 1814). During that war, the U.S. army bought meat from Samuel Wilson's meat market in Troy, New York. Sam Wilson was a friendly man, so people called him Uncle Sam. Uncle Sam always wrote the letters "U.S." on his boxes of meat for the army. The soldiers who ate Uncle Sam's meat began to call the U.S. government Uncle Sam. Soon, cartoons about Uncle Sam began to appear in newspapers in different states.

C   A hundred years later, the army used a picture of Uncle Sam on a poster to recruit soldiers for World War I (1914–1918). In the poster, Uncle Sam points his finger at the viewer and says: "I WANT YOU FOR U.S. Army."* After they saw this poster, many Americans called their government Uncle Sam. In other countries, too, Uncle Sam became a popular symbol of the United States.

D   As time passed, some Americans forgot the origin of the nickname Uncle Sam. Others heard the story about Sam Wilson, but didn't know if it was fact or folklore. To make it official, in 1961 the U.S. Congress declared that the name Uncle Sam came from the friendly meat man, Sam Wilson.

---

*The artist was James Montgomery Flagg.

After You Read

3. Look for Details   When did these events happen? Look at the time line below. Then scan the reading for the missing dates and write them on the lines provided. Compare answers with a partner.

1812	⇒	_____	⇒	_____	⇒	_____
Sam Wilson began to sell meat to the army.		U.S. soldiers ate the meat and called the U.S. Uncle Sam.		The army used a poster of Uncle Sam to recruit soldiers.		Congress said the nickname came from Sam Wilson.

4. Pick a Title   Work with a partner. Pick another title for the reading. The title gives the subject of the reading.

☐ **1.** Uncle Sam's Recruitment Poster

☐ **2.** The Origin of the Name 'Uncle Sam'

☐ **3.** The War of 1812

Discuss why the other two are not good titles.

5. Mark the Summary Scan the reading on page 45 and underline the sentence (or part of a sentence) that summarizes the reading. Compare answers with a partner.

6. Complete the Paragraph Use words from the box to complete the paragraph. Then listen to your instructor read the paragraph. Check your answers.

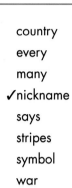

country
every
many
✓nickname
says
stripes
symbol
war

The Great Seal of the United States

Uncle Sam is just a _____nickname_____[1] for the United States government. The official _____[2] of the government is the Great Seal, which appears on _____[3] one-dollar bill. On this seal, a bald eagle holds an olive branch for peace, and thirteen arrows to show that the country is ready for _____[4] if necessary. In the eagle's beak is a scroll which _____[5] in Latin: *E Pluribus Unum*. This means "Out of Many Comes Unity," and represents one nation made up of _____[6] states. On the seal, thirteen red and white _____[7] represent the first thirteen states, and thirteen stars symbolize the birth of the _____.[8]

Listening Strategy
If you want your instructor to repeat a sentence, you can say: "Excuse me, would you please say that again?"

7. Write and Discuss   Look at the following drawings and captions. They show different views of the United States. Which ones do you think are true? On a separate sheet of paper, write a sentence to explain your reasons. Then discuss your opinions in small groups.

EXAMPLE: I think the United States is a peacekeeper because it helped bring peace to Bosnia.

1.   A Peacekeeper

2.   The World's Police

3.   A Leader in Science and Technology

4.   A Violent Nation

5.   A Rich Capitalist

6.   (Draw your own picture and write your own idea.)

A Snapshot of the United States

Before You Read

1. Take a Quiz   What do you already know about the United States? Work with a partner. Complete the following sentences by circling the letter of each correct answer.

Pacific Ocean

Atlantic Ocean

1. The first thirteen states were on the **a.** Atlantic Ocean. **b.** Pacific Ocean.	**4.** The U.S. was originally an **a.** industrial country. **b.** agricultural country.
2. The U.S. now has **a.** forty-eight states. **b.** fifty states.	**5.** Today, most Americans live **a.** on farms. **b.** in cities and suburbs.
3. The last state to join the U.S. was **a.** Hawaii. **b.** Puerto Rico.	**6.** Today, the U.S. population is about **a.** 150 million. **b.** 260 million.

While You Read

2. Look for Answers   While you read "A Snapshot of the United States" on page 49, check your answers to the quiz items in Exercise 1. Make changes, if necessary. Then compare answers with a partner.

A   Revolution created the United States, and change has been a part of its life ever since. The original thirteen British colonies along the Atlantic coast became the first thirteen states. The country quickly expanded across the Mississippi River and into the Great Plains. By the middle of the 1800s, the nation stretched as far as the Pacific Ocean. In 1959, Alaska and Hawaii became the forty-ninth and fiftieth states.

B   Originally, the United States was an agricultural country. Most Americans lived on farms. This rural way of life changed as the Industrial Revolution spread during the 1800s. Cities grew up around factories, as jobs drew people from the farms. After World War II (1939–1945), many city residents started moving to suburbs, smaller communities outside of cities. Today, about 78 percent of the U.S. population lives in cities and suburbs.

C   By the end of the twentieth century, the U.S. economy was changing again. This time it changed from a manufacturing economy (in which workers make products, such as cars or computers) to a service economy (in which workers provide a service, such as cooking or consulting). Many companies moved overseas, where workers' wages were lower. Other companies stayed in the U.S., but downsized, making their workforce smaller. As a result, many Americans lost their jobs or had to take lower paying jobs.

D   The U.S. population has also changed. It has grown from about 2 million in 1776 to about 260 million today. The earliest settlers were mainly white, Anglo-Saxon protestants. They came from Britain voluntarily. But there were involuntary immigrants, too. From 1619 to the late 1700s, about three hundred thousand Africans were brought in chains as slaves. In addition, about twenty thousand English prisoners were sent to America during the 1700s. They were sold as servants and had to work for seven years to get their freedom. Other immigrants from northern Europe followed, and in the late 1800s and early 1900s, immigrants from southern and eastern Europe began to arrive. Today, immigrants come from many countries, and the U.S. has become a multicultural society. In the future, one thing is certain—change will continue to be part of American life.

3. React to the Reading   On a separate sheet of paper, write your reaction to something that surprised or interested you in the reading. In small groups, share your reactions.

4. Look for Details   Scan the reading on page 49 for the missing details and write them in the table below. Compare answers with a partner.

Changes in the United States

	LATE 1700s	TODAY
Number of states:	13	
Type of economy:		
Population:		
Immigrants' homeland:		

5. Look for Definitions   Sometimes the meaning of a new word or words (or information about the word) can be found in the same sentence. The meaning often appears within parentheses or following a comma. Read the following sentence. Then answer the questions about the underlined words.

> After <u>World War II</u> (1939–1945), many city residents started moving to <u>suburbs</u>, smaller communities outside of cities.

1. What information about World War II is within parentheses? _____

2. What information about suburbs follows the comma? _____

6. Get the Meaning from Context   Work with a partner. Look at paragraph C of the reading. Find two examples of information within parentheses and one example of information following a comma. Write the new word or words on the lines provided in the left column. Then write the information about the words on the lines in the right column.

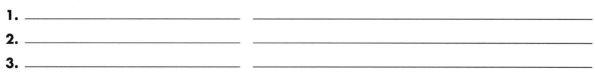

1. _____   _____

2. _____   _____

3. _____   _____

7. Identify Facts and Opinions Facts are true statements. Opinions are statements that some people believe—they may or may not be true. Work with a partner. Write *fact* or *opinion* next to each statement below.

EXAMPLE: _____*fact*_____ The U.S. population today is about 260 million.

_____*opinion*_____ The U.S. population is too large.

_____ **1.** The U.S. is made up of fifty states.

_____ **2.** Hawaii is the most beautiful state.

_____ **3.** The best place to live is in the suburbs.

_____ **4.** Most Americans live in cities and suburbs.

_____ **5.** A manufacturing economy is better than a service economy.

8. Write and Discuss Read **Just the Facts**. Then read the questions that follow and write your answers on a separate sheet of paper. Discuss your answers in small groups.

Just the Facts: Present and Future U.S. Population

Racial (or Ethnic) Group	Size in 1991	Expected* Size in 2041	Percent in 1991	Percent in 2041
Native Americans	2,000,000	2,000,000	.8%	.6%
Asian Americans	7,000,000	35,000,000	3%	10%
Hispanic Americans	21,000,000	64,000,000	9%	18%
African Americans	30,000,000	44,000,000	12%	12%
White Americans (non-Hispanic)	187,000,000	211,000,000	76%	59%

*Most of the increase in population will come from immigration.

Source: (based on) Crispell, Diane, "People Patterns." Wall Street Journal, March 16, 1992; Bl

1. In your own words, describe how the U.S. population will change. State facts and opinions.
2. Do any of the facts above surprise you? Which one(s)? Why?
3. Many future immigrants to the U.S. will not speak English. First, think about your own experiences with English. Then say what Uncle Sam should do to prepare immigrants for life in an English-speaking country.

Unit Two

Check Your Progress

You have just completed Unit Two. The following exercise reviews some information from Chapters 4–6. Compare answers with a partner.

Match the Information. Write the letters on the lines.

1. __j__ George Washington
2. _____ Betsy Ross
3. _____ Samuel Wilson
4. _____ James Hoban
5. _____ the Great Seal
6. _____ John Adams
7. _____ Jasper Johns
8. _____ Franklin Delano Roosevelt
9. _____ the Union Jack
10. _____ Dolley Madison

a. the architect who designed the White House

b. the first U.S. president to live in the White House

c. the only U.S. president to serve four consecutive terms

d. the flag of Great Britain

e. she saved George Washington's portrait

f. a meat merchant in New York

g. the official symbol of the United States

h. she made the first U.S. flag

i. he made paintings of the U.S. flag

j. the only U.S. president who didn't live in the White House

Follow Up

You can learn more about the topics in this unit by doing research and reporting your results to your class. You can also read books, and watch movies and videos about these topics. Here are some suggestions:

Chapter 4

Research and Report. Ask three people outside of class this question: *Do you think flag burning should be illegal?* Ask the people to give reasons for their answers. Take notes on their answers and write a summary. Report your findings to the class.

Chapter 5

Movies and Video. Watch one of these movies/videos in class or at home. Discuss your reactions.
Dave, a 1993 comedy, starring Kevin Klein
Mr. Smith Goes to Washington, a 1939 classic, starring James Stewart
Inside the White House, a 1989 guided tour (ABC Television)

Book. The following book about life in the White House was written by former First Lady, Barbara Bush.
Millie's Book, as dictated to Barbara Bush

Chapter 6

Research and Report. Ask three people outside of class the following question: *What does Uncle Sam mean to you?* Take notes on their answers. Report your findings to the class.

Education,
Architecture,
and Music

Do You Know . . .
- what percentage of people in the United States has a college degree?
- where the tallest building in the United States is?
- who the father of American folk music is?

In Unit Three, you will learn about some of the oldest universities in the United States. You will read about a city that is famous for its architecture and learn about electronic music.

Part One

The Ivy League

Before You Read

1. Discuss   Benjamin Franklin (1706–1790), a printer, inventor, statesman, and diplomat, wrote: "In Boston they ask, *How much does he know*? In New York, *How much is he worth*? In Philadelphia, *Who were his parents?*"
In small groups, discuss the following questions: What's most important in your country: education, money, or family background? How do you feel about this?

While You Read

2. Match Pictures and Paragraphs   Match three of the four paragraphs from the reading on page 55 with the pictures below. Compare answers with a partner.

1. _____

2. _____

3. _____

A   The Ivy League is the popular name for eight private colleges and universities in the northeastern part of the United States. They include Harvard University (established in 1636), Yale University (1701), the University of Pennsylvania (1740), Princeton University (1746), Columbia University (1754), Brown University (1764), Dartmouth College (1769), and Cornell University (1853). The name *Ivy League* comes from the ivy that typically grows up the walls of the schools' buildings.

B   The term *Ivy League,* however, means different things to different people. To some, Ivy League schools are elite institutions that have one purpose: to maintain the country's ruling class. To others, they are the pathway to top corporate and government jobs. Still others think of them as a way to gain prestige. In a society that values credentials, a diploma from an Ivy League school is impressive. Whatever one's opinion, it's clear that these schools have helped produce many of this country's leaders, including nine American presidents.

C   Since they were established, the Ivy League schools have tried to maintain their standards and traditions. But they have also heard the criticism against them and have changed with the times. Today, their student population is not made up of only wealthy, white, Protestant men, as it was in the past. While the tuition is still very expensive, today about half of the students receive some financial aid. While these schools began as all-male institutions, nearly half of the current students are women. And, while they have a reputation for being elitist, they now recruit the most capable students of all races, religious groups, and social classes. The political views of students in the past tended to be conservative, but recent polls show liberal leanings among most of the students and faculty.

D   One tradition that has not changed is that of alumni donations. Graduates are expected to support their schools by making annual cash donations. Ivy League schools do not receive government funds to educate their students. They must rely on tuition and their endowment, income mainly from alumni gifts. Graduates are expected to support future generations of students, just as past generations helped them enjoy the benefits of an Ivy League education: small class size, prominent professors, and the latest laboratory and research facilities. This tradition is one that the Ivy League schools are unlikely to change.

After You Read

3. Write a Summary   Choose one paragraph (B, C, or D) from the reading. On a separate sheet of paper, write a summary of the paragraph in your own words. Read the summary to your partner, and ask your partner for his or her reaction. Make any changes if necessary.

4. Look for Examples   Read the following main ideas. Then find at least one example in the reading to support each main idea. Compare answers with a partner.

1. The name *Ivy League* has different meanings for different people:

_____

2. Ivy League schools have changed some of their traditions:

_____

3. One tradition hasn't changed:

_____

5. Identify Facts and Opinions   Facts are true statements. Opinions are statements that some people believe—they may or may not be true. Work with a partner. Write *fact* or *opinion* next to each statement below.

EXAMPLE: _____*fact*_____ Brown University was established in 1764.

_____*opinion*_____ Harvard is the best university in the United States.

_____ **1.** The Ivy League schools are on the East coast.

_____ **2.** The buildings at the Ivy League schools are beautiful.

_____ **3.** It was a good idea for Ivy League schools to accept women.

_____ **4.** About half of the students at Ivy League schools get financial aid.

_____ **5.** Ivy League schools use money from tuition and their endowment to pay their bills.

6. Listen for Words in a List   As you listen to your instructor read the following three sentences, fill in the missing words.

Listening Strategy

If you want your instructor to repeat a particular word, you can say:
"Excuse me, what was the (second/next-to-last/last) (school/year/word)?"

---

1. The Ivy League schools include Harvard, _____, the University of Pennsylvania, Princeton, Columbia, Brown, _____, and _____.

2. The Ivy League schools were established in 1636, _____, 1740, 1746, 1754, 1764, _____, and _____.

3. In the past, the student population at Ivy League schools consisted of mainly wealthy, white, _____ men.

7. Look for Synonyms   A synonym is a word that has the same meaning as another word. Sometimes you can find a synonym for a new word in the same paragraph or in another paragraph. Read each sentence below from "The Ivy League." Then look in the reading for a synonym for each underlined word. Write the synonym on the line provided. Compare answers with a partner.

1. The <u>term</u> Ivy League, however, means different things to different people. (Look in paragraph A.)

_____.

2. One tradition that has not changed is that of alumni <u>donations</u>. (Look in paragraph D.)

_____

3. They must rely on tuition and their endowment, income mainly from <u>alumni</u> gifts. (Look in paragraph D.) _____

8. Complete the Conversation   Use words from the box to complete the conversation. Compare with a partner.

> established
> graduates
> institutions
> ✓ivy
> women

MAX: Did you know I went to Princeton University?

RICK: You're kidding! I didn't know you went to Princeton. When were you there?

MAX: Last weekend.

RICK: Oh, I thought you were a student there. So what's it like?

MAX: It's very pretty. There's a lot of _____ivy_____[1] growing up the walls of the buildings. Hey, did you know that two U.S. presidents were Princeton _____[2]? James Madison and Woodrow Wilson.

RICK: Is Princeton that old? Madison was president back in the early 1800s.

MAX: Yeah, it was _____[3] in 1746. You know, they didn't accept _____[4] until 1969!

RICK: Really? It was one of those all-male _____[5]? How boring!

9. Write and Discuss   On a separate sheet of paper, write your answers to the following questions. Then discuss your opinions in small groups.

1. Does your country value credentials, such as university diplomas, as much as the U.S. does? Are credentials a way of gaining prestige in your country?

2. In your country, is there a lot of competition to enter universities? If yes, do you think this is good or bad?

3. Is single-sex education (all-male or all-female) a good idea? Why or why not?

Part Two

Public Colleges

Before You Read

1. Take a Quiz   What do you already know about a university education in the United States? Work with a partner. Complete the following sentences by circling the correct answers.

1. The U.S. has about _____ colleges and universities.
   a. 250
   b. 2,500
2. Seven out of every ten college students in the U.S. study at a _____ college.
   a. private
   b. public
3. The first public universities in the U.S. were established for _____ people.
   a. upper-class
   b. working-class
4. In the U.S., more than half of all college freshmen are enrolled in _____ colleges.
   a. 2 year
   b. 4 year
5. Recent studies conclude that a university education is _____ to be successful today.
   a. necessary
   b. unnecessary

While You Read

2. Look for Answers   While you read "Public Colleges" on page 59, check your answers to the quiz items in Exercise 1. Make changes, if necessary. Then compare answers with a partner.

A   James Madison, the fourth president, warned that "a well-instructed people alone can be permanently a free people." Not long after Madison's presidency, in 1832, the French writer Alexis de Tocqueville toured the United States. He found that education prepared Americans to participate in the governing of their country. He said this participation made democracy a success in the U.S. In his book *Democracy in America,* de Tocqueville also noted that the U.S. had more schools than other countries. At the university level, de Tocqueville's observation is still true today. There are more than 2,500 colleges and universities nationwide.

B   During Madison and de Tocqueville's time, higher education was in private hands. Today, seven out of every ten students in higher education attend a public school. How did this happen? In 1862, the U.S. Congress gave the states permission to sell government land and use the money to establish colleges. These "land-grant colleges," were designed for the working class. They emphasized practical subjects like agriculture, engineering, and military science.

C   In the first half of the twentieth century, public institutions from the University of California to the City University of New York educated the children of immigrants and the urban poor. Many graduates became leaders in their fields. But without public universities, they might never have received an education. In the second half of the twentieth century, public colleges and universities educated large numbers of women, African Americans, and immigrants. These groups were traditionally not well represented in college. Public schools have become truly public. They exist for the people and are paid for by the people—through taxes and a modest tuition, along with donations from alumni and corporations.

D   More recently, community colleges have become the fastest-growing segment of public education. More than half of all college freshmen are enrolled in these two-year schools. Like the original land-grant colleges, community colleges offer job training at a reasonable cost. Because community colleges are located right in the community, they make a college education possible for students who must live at home and work while they attend school.

E   Several studies at the end of the twentieth century conclude that higher education is necessary to get ahead in our modern world. Both sophisticated jobs and a democratic system demand it, as Madison and de Tocqueville observed. Parents in the U.S. have always wanted their children to have a better life than they had. For many young people, public colleges and universities offer the only chance to reach that goal.

3. React to the Reading On a separate sheet of paper, write your reaction to something that surprised or interested you in the reading. Then, in small groups, share your reactions.

4. Check the Topics Check all the topics below that are presented in the reading. Then write the letter of the corresponding paragraph after each topic checked off. Compare answers with a partner.

TOPICS	PARAGRAPH LETTER
☐ **1.** the origin of "land-grant colleges"	_____
☐ **2.** the importance of education in a democracy	_____
☐ **3.** studies on the importance of a college education	_____
☐ **4.** the subjects taught in four-year public colleges today	_____
☐ **5.** special features of community colleges	_____
☐ **6.** the student population at public institutions in the 1900s	_____
☐ **7.** James Madison's education at Princeton University	_____

5. Pick the Summary Read the following summaries. Then check the one that best summarizes the reading on page 59.

☐ **1.** Community colleges are popular because they offer job training, and the tuition is not very expensive.

☐ **2.** Community colleges and other public institutions of higher education have made a college education possible for many young people in the U.S. Some of these schools started out as land-grant colleges for the working class.

☐ **3.** Studies show that a college education is becoming a necessity for those who want to be successful.

6. Say What to Do In each situation below, say what to do. Use information from the reading, and write your answers on the lines provided. Then compare answers with a partner.

1. To learn more about de Tocqueville's observations of the U.S.,

_____

2. For a two-year college education in your neighborhood,

_____

3. To get additional income, public institutions should

_____

7. Complete the Conversation   Use words from the box to complete the conversation. Compare answers with a partner.

> African   century   goals   home   nationwide   practical   public   work

TINA: I think I want to go to Oberlin College.

YOKO: That's in Ohio, isn't it? I guess you're not going to live at
_____.[1] Why do you want to go there?

TINA: Oberlin was a leader in educating women and _____[2]
Americans. Did you know that in the middle of the nineteenth
_____[3] it was one of only two colleges
_____[4] that admitted women? The other was Mount
Holyoke College.

YOKO: Is Oberlin a _____[5] or a private college?

TINA: Private.

YOKO: What are you going to study?

TINA: Something _____[6] like computer science. I want to
_____[7] and make some money when I graduate. I have
_____.[8]

8. Write and Discuss   Read **Just the Facts**. Then read the questions that follow and write your answers on a separate sheet of paper. Discuss your answers in small groups.

Just the Facts: Education of Adults (25 years and over) in the U.S.

SCHOOLING	PERCENTAGE OF THE POPULATION
1–8 years (elementary school)	10.6%
9–11 years (some high school)	11.0%
12 years, high school graduate (no college)	38.6%
13–15 years (1–3 years of college)	18.4%
16 years or more (college graduate or more)	21.4%

Source: Based on U.S. Bureau of the Census, 1991

1. What general statements can you make about the statistics above? Do any of them surprise you?
2. What should colleges do: help students develop a love of learning or help them prepare for a job? Why?
3. Do you agree with President Madison that, to be permanently free, a population must be well educated? Why or why not?

CHAPTER 8

Part One

The Wright Architecture

Before You Read

1. Interview and Draw   Interview your partner about his or her dream house. Try to draw it. Then share your drawing with the class.

While You Read

2. Write Captions   Using information from the reading, write captions (descriptions) under the pictures below. Compare captions with a partner.

1.   Frank Lloyd Wright

_____

_____

_____

2.   The Robie House in Illinois is one of Wright's famous private houses.

3.   The Prairie Houses

_____

_____

_____

4.   The Imperial Hotel

_____

_____

_____

5.   The Guggenheim Museum

_____

_____

_____

6.   The Convention Center

_____

_____

_____

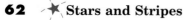

A   One of the leading American architects of the twentieth century was Frank Lloyd Wright. His designs delighted some and bothered others. But his influence on architecture continued throughout the century.

B   Wright was born on a farm in Wisconsin in 1867. As a child, he played with toys created by Friedrich Froebel, a German teacher who developed kindergarten education. Later, Wright said he learned about shapes and colors from these toys. At the University of Wisconsin, he studied engineering. He taught himself architecture, because there was no architecture program. One of his first architectural jobs was in Chicago, where he worked with the famous architect Louis Sullivan.

C   His career lasted seventy years. He designed a variety of buildings but is probably best known for his private houses. These include his own home—now called the Frank Lloyd Wright House—the Dana House, and the Robie House, all in Illinois. He rejected the traditional design of a home with rooms placed symmetrically on each side of a hall and central staircase. Instead, he created a flow of space. His rooms flowed from a central area with a large living room. His houses were low and horizontal like the flat Midwestern landscape. With his Prairie Houses (1900–1915) and Usonian Houses (1939–1959), Wright developed a style based on comfort, convenience, and open spaces. He used inexpensive, mass-produced materials. His architecture was new, economical, and Midwestern.

D   Wright's houses were influenced by Japanese architectural design, and all his projects outside North America were in Japan. In Tokyo, he created the Imperial Hotel, which became a legend. Shortly after the hotel opened, an earthquake destroyed one-third of Tokyo. Wright's hotel remained standing, and the architect became known as a master builder.

E   Until recently, Wright's last masterpiece was the Guggenheim Museum in New York City. It was designed in the shape of a seashell. Visitors take an elevator to the top, then spiral down a continuous space. But now there is one more Frank Lloyd Wright building. It's a convention center in his boyhood town, Madison, Wisconsin. It was designed in 1958, but Wright's opponents blocked its construction. Today, on the shore of Lake Monona, so many years after Wright's death, his work continues to delight some and bother others.

After You Read

3. Read in Groups of Words   Read the example below. Then circle each group of words in the reading. When you finish, read it again silently in groups of words.

EXAMPLE: (One of the leading American architects of the twentieth century)

(was Frank Lloyd Wright.)

4. React to the Reading and Pictures   Do you like Wright's buildings? Why or why not? On a separate sheet of paper, write your reaction to Wright's designs. Use the pictures, the reading, or other information you have about Wright's designs. In small groups, share your reactions.

5. Figure It Out   The first paragraph says that Wright's designs bothered some people. In other words, some people didn't like the designs. The reading doesn't explain why Wright's designs bothered people. Using information from the reading, can you figure out why? Write your answer on the lines provided. Then compare answers with a partner.

_____

_____

_____

6. Look for Examples   Read the following main ideas. Then find at least one example in the reading to support each main idea. Compare answers with a partner.

1.   One of the leading American architects of the twentieth century was Frank Lloyd Wright.

_____

2.   He is probably best known for his private houses.

_____

3.   His architecture was new, economical, and Midwestern.

_____

4.   Over the years, his designs delighted some and bothered others.

_____

7. Complete the Story   Use words from the box to complete the story. Compare answers with a partner.

architect
design
influence
influenced
own
✓private
space

One of Frank Lloyd Wright's _____private_____[1] houses, the Warren Hickox House (1900), is a good example of his Prairie Houses. These were _____[2] by Japanese _____.[3] Some say the roof is like Japanese folding screens. Wooden trim forms bands of color against the stucco walls. Inside there is a continuous flow of _____.[4]

The _____[5] loved Japanese works of art, too. In his _____[6] home, he wanted to have only Japanese prints, sculpture, and ceramics. But Wright was a strange person. He claimed the Japanese did not _____[7] his work.

8. Write and Discuss   On a separate sheet of paper, write your answers to the following questions. Then discuss your opinions in small groups.

1. What do contemporary houses look like in your country? Do you like them? Why or why not?
2. Many famous people say that something from their childhood influenced their choice of career. For example, Wright was influenced by the creative toys of Froebel that taught him about shapes and colors. What would you give or show your children to influence them? Here are some possibilities: building blocks, books, music, trips, television shows. Be specific.
3. Was there something from your childhood that influenced your career choice or goals? What was it? How did it influence you?

Part Two

The Architectural Capital of the Country

Before You Read

1. Plan a Trip In small groups, decide which city in the United States your group would like to visit. Make a list of what you would like to do there—visit skyscrapers, visit art museums, go to the theater, go shopping, eat in certain restaurants, and so on. Decide when you would like to make your trip and how you will travel. Use the outline below to present your plan to the class.

City: _____

When to travel: _____

How to travel: _____

PLACES TO VISIT:

_____

_____

_____

_____

_____

THINGS TO DO:

_____

_____

_____

_____

_____

While You Read

2. Mark the Text Look for the topic of each paragraph of the reading on page 67. Remember that the topic is the subject of the paragraph. Write "T" for the topic in the left margin. The following are some examples of topics from the previous reading, "The Wright Architecture."

A. one of the leading architects of the twentieth century
B. Wright's childhood and training
C. how Wright's houses were different from traditional designs
D. how Wright became a legend in Japan
E. Wright's last two buildings

Compare answers with a partner.

A   Why are buildings designed a particular way: to please the eye or to serve a purpose? What is the focus of a design: form or function? Ideally, buildings are designed to serve both. In this country, one city has led the rest in architecture that is new in both form and function. That city is Chicago, the architectural capital of the United States.

B   But why Chicago? It started in 1871 with a cow in Mrs. O'Leary's barn. According to legend, Catherine O'Leary was milking her cow and using a lantern to light the barn. The cow kicked over the lantern and started a fire.* The barn was near the business district, and the fire spread quickly to that area. It jumped the Chicago River and burned the water-pumping station. This made it impossible to pump water to fight the flames. Rain finally put out the fire after two days. In the end, the fire destroyed eighteen thousand buildings, killed three hundred people, and left one hundred thousand people homeless.

C   After the Great Fire, much of the city's business district had to be rebuilt. A building boom followed. Within a year, three thousand buildings went up. Chicago architects Louis Sullivan, Daniel H. Burnham, William Le Baron Jenney, and others redesigned much of downtown Chicago. It was this architecture boom that drew Frank Lloyd Wright to Chicago in 1887. Just two years earlier, the world's first steel-frame skyscraper was built—the Home Insurance Building. It was only nine stories tall, but the idea spread to cities around the world.

D   Today, the tallest building in the U.S., the 110-story Sears Tower, is also in Chicago. It is part of the Magnificent Mile. This mile of Michigan Avenue is an important business center and shopping area. It includes much of the city's most modern architecture. Today, that means tall, *very* tall. In addition to the Sears Tower, the Magnificent Mile also offers the one-hundred story John Hancock Center, called Big John. An observatory on the ninety-fourth floor provides views of the city and Lake Michigan. Not far from Big John is Big Stan, the eighty-story Standard Oil building (now owned by the American Oil Company AMOCO).

E   For over a century, Chicago has led the nation in innovative skyscrapers. But why build such huge towers? Some say it's the best way to use expensive real estate. Some say it's a big advertisement for the corporation that owns the building. Others consider it a symbol of pride for city residents. Still others call it a monument to the architect. Architectural ideas continue to change, blending old and new, blending form and function, and bringing novelty to the urban landscape. What new ideas will the twenty-first century bring?

---

*In 1997, over one hundred years after the Great Fire, Mrs. O'Leary and her cow were cleared of blame. It is now believed that the fire was started by her son, Daniel Sullivan, who was carelessly smoking in the barn.

3. Match Pictures and Descriptions The following are the six tallest skyscrapers in the U.S. They are all in Chicago or New York City. Using information from the reading and any information you may already have, fill in the missing details below (the city and number of stories). Then match the pictures and the descriptions by writing the letter of the building that corresponds to each picture. Compare answers with a partner.

a. Sears Tower, _____Chicago_____, ___110___ stories, (1,454 feet/443 meters)

b. World Trade Center, _____, 110 stories, (1,377 feet/419 meters)

c. Empire State Building, _____, 102 stories, (1,250 feet/381 meters)

d. John Hancock Center, _____, _____ stories, (1,136 feet/346 meters)

e. AMOCO Building, _____, _____ stories, (1,127 feet/343 meters)

f. Chrysler Building, _____, 77 stories, (1,046 feet/305 meters)

1. _____

2. __A__

3. _____

4. _____

5. _____

6. _____

4. Pick the Summary   Read the following summaries. Then check the one that best summarizes the reading. Compare answers with a partner.

☐ **1.** After the Great Fire of 1871, much of downtown Chicago had to be rebuilt. Soon the country's first skyscraper went up, blending form and function. Chicago became the architecture capital of the United States.

☐ **2.** In 1871, an accident in Mrs. O'Leary's barn caused the Great Fire in Chicago. The fire destroyed eighteen thousand buildings, killed three hundred people, and left one hundred thousand people homeless.

☐ **3.** The architecture boom in Chicago after the Great Fire of 1871 drew Frank Lloyd Wright to that city.

5. Write and Discuss   Read **Just the Facts**. Then read the questions that follow and write your answers on a separate sheet of paper. Discuss your answers in small groups.

Just the Facts: Architecture, Frank Lloyd Wright, and Chicago

- Frank Lloyd Wright's Ennis-Brown House in Los Angeles has appeared in several movies, starting with the 1933 film *Female*. More recently, the house was in *Blade Runner, House on Haunted Hill,* and *Day of the Locust*.

- Chicago's nickname, the Windy City, does not refer to the weather. New York newspapers used the name in the 1890s to refer to Chicagoans' boastfulness.

- Sixty thousand people move to Chicago each year. One sixth of them are immigrants.

- The Sears Tower was the tallest building in the world until the Petronas Towers were built in Kuala Lumpur, Malaysia. The towers have only eighty-eight stories, but they are 1,476 feet tall.

1. What's more important to you—the way a building looks (its form), or the purpose it serves (its function)? For example, one purpose may be to provide offices for a large number of companies in a small space. A different purpose might be to integrate a home into its environment.

2. A number of skyscrapers have recently been built (or are being built) in Malaysia, China, Hong Kong, and Taiwan. Why do you think these huge towers are going up?

3. What are the alternatives to building skyscrapers in downtown areas?

4. Which city in your country has famous architecture? Why is the architecture famous?

CHAPTER 9

Part One

This Land Is Your Land

Before You Read

1. Interview First, write your own answers to the following survey questions. Then interview your partner and write his or her answers. Discuss your answers with your partner.

Entertainment and Music Survey

MY ANSWERS:

1. What do you do in your free time?

☐ watch television

☐ read

☐ listen to music

☐ go to movies, concerts, etc.

2. What kind of music do you like?

☐ classical   ☐ popular music

☐ country   ☐ jazz

☐ rock   ☐ blues

☐ rap   ☐ folk

MY PARTNER'S ANSWERS:

1. What do you do in your free time?

☐ watch television

☐ read

☐ listen to music

☐ go to movies, concerts, etc.

2. What kind of music do you like?

☐ classical   ☐ popular music

☐ country   ☐ jazz

☐ rock   ☐ blues

☐ rap   ☐ folk

While You Read

2. Describe a Drawing Think about a drawing that would illustrate the most important idea in each paragraph of the reading on page 71. On a separate sheet of paper, describe each drawing. Then compare answers with a partner.

Paragraph A: <u>Woody Guthrie as a boy growing up in Oklahoma</u>

A   The folksinger Woody Guthrie was born in a small town in Oklahoma in 1912. He was named Woodrow Wilson Guthrie after the man who was elected President of the United States that year, Woodrow Wilson. Despite his distinguished name, life wasn't easy for young Woody Guthrie. His house burned down, his sister died in an accident, and his father's business went bankrupt. His mother was sent to a mental institution. By age 15, Woody had no family left.

B   In the 1930s, the Great Depression (an economic crisis) and a terrible drought (a period with no rain) made life even more difficult for Woody Guthrie and all Oklahomans. During the drought, wind picked up the dry soil, creating dust storms. Whole buildings were buried, and farms were ruined. The region became known as the Dust Bowl. Many people, including Woody Guthrie, left the Dust Bowl to find work in California. For Guthrie, it was the beginning of an endless journey.

C   He traveled the country by freight train with only a guitar and a harmonica. There was a sharpness to his voice and his message, but people welcomed him everywhere. He sang at parties, at rodeos, in bars, and at home. Home was usually a friend's apartment, a cheap hotel, the back seat of a car, or a freight train.

D   Woody Guthrie couldn't read music, but he wrote more than one thousand songs. Some of his songs ("So Long, It's Been Good to Know You" and "Worried Man Blues") became American classics. During the Great Depression, Guthrie sang about working people, poor people, and hungry people. But they were happy, optimistic songs. Guthrie said, "I hate a song that makes you think you're not any good."

E   In 1940, he recorded his first album in New York City. It was called *Dust Bowl Ballads.* The songs were about hard times living in and leaving the Dust Bowl. As Guthrie's ballads became popular from coast to coast, people in the music business began to tell him what to do. He didn't like it and walked out. He didn't want money, and he didn't want fame—he wanted to be free.

F Woody Guthrie died in New York City in 1967, but many of his folk songs are still sung today. One of his most popular songs shows his love for the land he traveled across. It's called "This Land Is Your Land." In the 1960s, it was adopted by the civil rights movement. Here are the first four lines:

> This land is your land, this land is my land
> From California to the New York island,
> From the Redwood Forest to the Gulf Stream waters
> This land was made for you and me.©

G Guthrie influenced his contemporaries like Pete Seeger and many younger folksingers, especially Bob Dylan. In a *Tribute to Woody Guthrie*, Dylan, Joan Baez, Judy Collins, Richie Havens, Woody Guthrie's son, Arlo Guthrie, and others recorded Guthrie songs. Arlo Guthrie followed in his father's footsteps and became a successful folksinger and songwriter, too. Thirty years after his father's death, he recorded a collection of his father's songs for children. It's called *Woody's 20 Grow Big Songs*.

After You Read

3. Write a Summary   Choose paragraphs A, B, and C or D, E, F, and G from the reading. On a separate sheet of paper, write a summary of the paragraphs in your own words. Read the summary to your partner, and ask your partner for his or her reaction. Make any changes if necessary.

4. Identify Stated or Implied Information   Some information is stated directly in the story. Other information is implied; it is not stated directly. Details in the reading suggest that it's true. Work with a partner. Write *stated* or *implied* next to each sentence below.

EXAMPLE: _____stated_____   Woody Guthrie was named after a president.

_____implied_____   The Dust Bowl had a strong effect on Woody Guthrie.

_____ **1.** As a young man, Woody Guthrie had a difficult life.

_____ **2.** Woody Guthrie traveled around the U.S. with only a few possessions.

_____ **3.** Woody Guthrie was a very talented songwriter.

_____ **4.** Woody Guthrie got married and had a family.

_____ **5.** Woody Guthrie didn't want to be rich and famous.

5. Complete the Conversation   Use words from the box to complete the conversation. Compare answers with a partner.

business
classics
folk
✓ guitar
influenced
popular
songwriters

SUSAN: I see jazz, country, rock, and rap music, but no section for

_____[1] music. I don't understand.

ANNA: It's not that _____[2] anymore. I think it's mixed in with the

country music section.

SUSAN: I don't understand people in the music _____[3] Folk was

big. People like Woody Guthrie _____[4] a whole generation

of singers and _____[5] Guthrie wrote songs that became

American _____[6]

ANNA: I guess people want more than a simple ___guitar___[7] and a

harmonica.

SUSAN: Yeah, they want noise!

6. Write and Discuss   On a separate sheet of paper, write your answers to the following questions. Then discuss your opinions in small groups.

1. Do you like songs that have a message—a special point they are trying to make? Why or why not? Give examples of songs like this.
2. Like Woody Guthrie, many people in the United States think personal freedom is important. Is personal freedom important in your country? Is it important to you?
3. Why do you think Woody Guthrie's songs were so popular?

Part Two

Techno Land

Before You Read

1. Take a Quiz   What do you already know about techno music? Work with a partner. Complete the following sentences by circling the letter of each correct answer.

1. Techno is electronic music
   a. to listen to.
   b. to dance to.
2. The name *techno* comes from the word
   a. technology.
   b. technique.
3. Techno music uses
   a. drum machines.
   b. real drummers.
4. Techno music doesn't use
   a. humans.
   b. human voices.
5. Raves are
   a. all-night dance parties.
   b. daytime dance parties.
6. People who like techno music want to
   a. have fun.
   b. help others.

While You Read

2. Look for Answers   While you read "Techno Land" on page 75, check your answers to the quiz items in Exercise 1. Make changes if necessary. Then compare answers with a partner.

A   If Woody Guthrie were alive today, he would probably be shocked and disappointed to learn about techno music. It's a far cry from the simple sounds of Guthrie's guitar, harmonica, and voice. Techno is electronic dance music. It has a relentless drum beat that is created by drum machines instead of a drummer. It typically uses a lot of short samples (small parts) of the songs of other recording artists. Popular techno groups include the Chemical Brothers, Orbital, the Prodigy, Model 500, Altern 8, and Program 2. But techno music usually does not include human voices. When it does, the voice chants or screeches a phrase over and over. The effect on the dancers is intended to be hypnotic.

B   Techno-heads—followers of techno music and techno groups—listen to loud techno music at all-night dance parties called *raves*. Raves are open to the public and can be small, with fifty people, or large, with thousands. Whatever the number, the point is to escape the problems of everyday life through music and dance.

C   At a rave, the deejay (disc jockey) is supposed to be the creative force. It's the deejay's job to know the music, especially the beats per minute, and to create a continuous stream of dance music. When they're good, deejays themselves can develop a following. In some cases, the deejay is more popular than the members of the techno groups. But techno has a do-it-yourself quality. With the cost of drum machines and sampler technology going down, almost anybody can produce techno music.

D   Techno (also called *electronica* and *electro*) can range from Detroit techno, with a pounding rhythm and no vocals, to hard-core techno and techno rave, with a softer style and occasional vocals. Ambient is the only type of techno music that's not for dancing. It's electronic music to sit and listen to.

E   Unlike many music lovers of the 1960s and 1970s, techno-heads are not usually concerned with politics or social issues. Unlike Woody Guthrie during the Depression, they don't seem to care about the problems of the poor and unfortunate. Techno-heads are pleasure seekers. They want to forget everything, feel the music, and, most of all, have fun.

F   With no melody to hum, can techno attract many followers? Is techno a serious development in music or just a fad that will disappear shortly? Is it a reflection of the fast-paced, often impersonal life we lead at the end of the twentieth and the beginning of the twenty-first century? Does it reflect, for some, a feeling of frustration with the world? How does techno compare to Woody Guthrie's response to the challenges of his time? Fifty years from now, will people find inspiration in techno music as many still do in Woody Guthrie's music?

3. Read in Groups of Words Read the example below. Then circle each group of words in the reading. When you finish, read it again silently in groups of words.

EXAMPLE: (If Woody Guthrie were alive today,)

(he would probably be shocked and disappointed)

(to learn about techno music.)

4. React to the Reading On a separate sheet of paper, write your reaction to something that surprised or interested you in the reading. Then, in small groups, share your reactions.

5. Look for the Point of View What is the author's point of view in "Techno Land"? Is she for or against techno music? How do you know? Discuss these questions with a partner. Then share your answers in small groups.

6. Check the Topics Check all the topics below that are presented in the reading. Then write the letter of the corresponding paragraph after each topic checked off. Compare answers with a partner.

TOPICS	PARAGRAPH LETTER
☐ **1.** the meaning of *techno-heads* and *raves*	_____
☐ **2.** questions about techno music	_____
☐ **3.** how techno first developed	_____
☐ **4.** what techno music is and who the groups are	_____
☐ **5.** the different types of techno music	_____
☐ **6.** what techno-heads are concerned with	_____
☐ **7.** the role of the deejay in techno music	_____
☐ **8.** the most popular techno songs	_____

7. Say What to Do For each situation below, say what to do. Using information from the reading, write your answers on the lines provided. Then compare answers with a partner.

1. If you want to dance all night, forget the world's problems, and have fun,

_____

2. If you don't like to dance, but you want to listen to techno music,

_____

3. If you like techno music and you have your own drum machine and sampler,

_____

8. Write and Discuss Read **Just the Facts**. Then read the questions that follow and write your answers on a separate sheet of paper. Discuss your answers in small groups.

Just the Facts: Music

- 450,000 people attended Woodstock—a festival of folk and rock music— near Bethel, New York, for three days and nights in August 1969.

- More than four hundred thousand fans attended a reunion concert by the folk singers and songwriters Paul Simon and Art Garfunkel in New York City in September 1981.

- The 1985 song "We Are the World" was written and performed by famous pop musicians to help the people of Africa. It earned more than 30 million dollars.

- In the early 1990s, rock 'n' roll fell behind rap and country music in popularity.

1. Why do you think folk music and rock 'n' roll have fallen in popularity?
2. Do you think musicians should join together to support social causes through concerts or recordings?
3. What is the most popular music in your country? Who are the most popular performers?

Unit Three

Check Your Progress

You have just completed Unit Three. The following exercise reviews some information from Chapters 7–9. Do this exercise, then compare answers with a partner.

1. In which part of the United States are the Ivy League schools located?
   a. the northwest **b.** the southeast **c.** the northeast **d.** the midwest
2. Which university is not an Ivy League school?
   a. Harvard **b.** Brown **c.** Columbia **d.** Wisconsin
3. More than half of all college freshmen attend
   a. private schools **b.** two-year colleges
   c. four-year colleges **d.** Ivy League schools
4. Which of the following buildings was *not* designed by Frank Lloyd Wright?
   a. Warren Hickox House **b.** the Guggenheim Museum
   c. Sears Tower **d.** the Imperial Hotel
5. The tallest building in the United States is _____.
   a. the Sears Tower **b.** the World Trade Center
   c. the John Hancock Tower **d.** the Empire State Building
6. Woody Guthrie was named after a famous _____.
   a. folksinger **b.** president of the United States **c.** architect **d.** writer
7. Which of these singers was influenced by Woody Guthrie?
   a. Bob Dylan **b.** Joan Baez **c.** Pete Seeger **d.** Answers *a*, *b*, and *c*
8. In what way(s) is techno music different from the folk music of Woody Guthrie?
   a. It is electronic. **b.** It is dance music.
   c. It has a strong drum beat. **d.** Answers *a*, *b*, and *c*

Follow Up

You can learn more about these topics by doing research and reporting information to your class. You can also read books and watch movies about these topics. Here are some suggestions.

Chapter 7

Research and Report. Interview three people outside of class. Ask them these questions: *Did you go to a private or public college/university? Which school was it? Would you recommend your school to others?* Take notes on their answers and write a summary. Report back to your class.

Chapter 8

Research and Report. Choose a building you like very much. Research its architect and style of architecture. Report your findings to the class.

Chapter 9

Movies and Videos. Watch one of these movies/videos in class or at home. Discuss your reactions.
Woody Guthrie: Hard Times Travelin', a musical tribute
Bound for Glory, a film based on Woody Guthrie's autobiography

Book. *Bound for Glory* by Woody Guthrie.

History

Do You Know . . .
- where the Museum of African American History is?
- who the first European to sail to the Americas was?
- the latest research about the first Americans?

In Unit Four, you will learn about the causes of the Civil War in the United States and about the struggle of African Americans to gain their freedom. You will also read about Christopher Columbus's voyages to the Americas and about how Native Americans have fought for survival in the United States.

CHAPTER 10

Part One

The Causes of the Civil War

Before You Read

1. Discuss The map below shows the United States in 1861, the year the Civil War began. Work with a partner. Look at the map and discuss the questions. (Note: The word *territory* on the map means that this area was not a state.)

1. How many states did the United States have in 1861?
2. The top half of the map shows the Northern part of the country, and the bottom half shows the Southern part. What difference does the map show between the Northern and Southern states?

The United States in 1861

- ▨ Free state
- ☐ Territory
- ▨ Slave state

While You Read

2. Take Notes Take notes while you read "The Causes of the Civil War," on pages 81 and 82. List the causes of the Civil War. When you finish, compare notes with a partner.

The Causes of the Civil War

_____

_____

_____

A   America's Civil War (1861–1865) was a bloody struggle between the Northern states and the Southern states. About 620,000 soldiers died in the war. What were the causes? How did the country come to be so divided?

B   When the thirteen colonies declared their independence from Great Britain and formed a new government in 1789, they disagreed on several issues. One issue was states' rights: Which powers should stay with the states, and which powers should be given to the federal (national) government? Another issue was slavery—owning people who must work without pay. Northerners, for many reasons, were against slavery. Although only one in four southerners owned slaves, most southerners felt slavery was necessary for their agricultural way of life.

C   As the new country expanded westward, the issue of slavery followed. In 1819, when Missouri applied for admission to the Union as a slave state, people in the North opposed this. Northerners had moral, economic, and political reasons to stop the spread of slavery. Some northerners felt that slavery was morally wrong, especially in a country that valued freedom. (They were called abolitionists because they wanted to abolish—or end—slavery.) Others, mainly poor whites, were against slavery for economic reasons. They saw opportunities to make money in the west. How could they get well-paid work if slaves could do the same job for free? Still others had political problems with slavery. At the time, there were eleven slave states and eleven free states. If Missouri joined the country as a slave state, that would change the balance of power in the United States Senate. The issue came up again and again as the country grew. In 1846, a Pennsylvania Congressman suggested a law that would make *all* new states free states. Fistfights broke out in the House of Representatives and, in the territories, the struggle over slavery turned bloody.

D   Other developments, too, fanned the political fires. One was an economic depression, mainly in the north, in 1857 and 1858. Northerners wanted to increase tariffs (taxes) to help struggling businesses, but Southerners didn't support these increases.

E   In 1857, a Supreme Court decision further divided the country. A slave named Dred Scott claimed his freedom when his owner moved him from a slave state to a free state. After years in state courts, his case went to the United States Supreme Court. At the time, most of the Court's justices were southerners. They dismissed the case because only citizens could sue in the federal courts. Since Dred Scott was black, and blacks were not citizens, he could not use the federal courts. The Court also ruled that the federal government did not have the power to make decisions on the movement of property (in this case, a slave) in the territories. The Court said that this was an issue for the states to decide. This decision angered many northerners. They thought it was an issue to be decided by the federal government, not the states.

F   As one political battle followed another, Congressmen stopped voting with their political party and voted with the North or the South. Southern leaders threatened to secede from—or leave—the Union. In their view, the United States was a voluntary union, and they could leave that union, just as the colonies had seceded from England.

G   In the presidential election of 1860, Abraham Lincoln and his Republican Party were against slavery in the new territories. They were also against the breakup of the Union. Lincoln argued that democracy was not possible if a small group of states could leave the national government any time there was a disagreement. Many southerners were afraid of a Lincoln presidency because of his promise to abolish slavery. When members of South Carolina's legislature heard that Lincoln had been elected President of the United States, they voted to secede from the Union. In January, 1861, six more Southern states—Mississippi, Florida, Alabama, Georgia, Louisiana, and Texas—followed South Carolina. In February, 1861, the seven states formed the Confederate States of America. Later four more states—Virginia, Arkansas, Tennessee, and North Carolina—joined the Confederacy.*

H   Sadly, the years of debate over the issues of slavery and states' rights vs. federal supremacy found no solution. In the end, the issues were decided by a bloody civil war. The country was torn apart and much of the South was destroyed, but the Union—under Lincoln's leadership—survived, and slavery was abolished.

---

*Four slave states—Delaware, Maryland, Kentucky, and Missouri—decided not to secede. West Virginia separated from Virginia (a slave state), to become a nonslave state. It was admitted to the Union in 1863.

After You Read

3. React to the Reading   On a separate sheet of paper, write your reaction to something that surprised or interested you in the reading. Then, in small groups, share your reactions.

4. Look for Details   Three of the issues that led to the Civil War are given below. The reading gives the views of the North and South on each issue. Work with a partner. Fill in the chart below with these views.

	North	**South**
slavery in new states		
movement of property in new territories		
the breakup of the Union		

5. Look for Definitions   Sometimes the meaning of a new word can be found in the same sentence, after a dash (—), or inside parentheses. Find each word below in the reading. (The letter after each word shows the paragraph it is in.) Then write the definitions of those words.

1. federal (B) _____

2. slavery (B) _____

3. abolish (C) _____

4. abolitionists (C) _____

5. tariffs (D) _____

6. secede (F) _____

6. Complete the Paragraph   Use words from the box to complete the story. Compare answers with a partner.

abolitionist   died   freedom   North   slavery   slaves   ✓wrong

John Brown's Raid on Harper's Ferry

John Brown was an extreme _____,[1] a man who believed slavery was

_____wrong_____[2] and wanted to end it. He had an idea that he could stop

_____[3] by starting a slave rebellion. Brown believed that if he could

give guns to _____,[4] they would fight for their _____.[5]

To get guns, Brown and a group of eighteen followers attacked and captured the United

States arsenal (a place where guns and bullets are kept) at Harper's Ferry, Virginia, on

October 16, 1859. Eight men _____,[6] including two of Brown's sons.

Brown was captured and hanged. Many people in the _____[7] protested

his execution.

Part Two

The Road to Freedom

Before You Read

1. Interview   First, write your own answers to the following interview questions. Then interview your partner and write his or her answers. Discuss your answers with your partner.

Discrimination Interview

In many countries, one group of people treats another group badly because of its race, nationality, religion, sexual orientation, or other characteristic. This is called *discrimination* or *prejudice*.

MY ANSWERS:

1.   Is it possible to end discrimination?

☐ yes   ☐ no

2.   What is the best way to try to end discrimination?

☐ demonstrations

☐ new laws

☐ education

☐ court cases

☐ other: _____

MY PARTNER'S ANSWERS:

1.   Is it possible to end discrimination?

☐ yes   ☐ no

2.   What is the best way to try to end discrimination?

☐ demonstrations

☐ new laws

☐ education

☐ court cases

☐ other: _____

While You Read

2. Write Captions   Using information from the reading on pages 85 and 86, write captions (descriptions) under the pictures below. Compare captions with a partner.

1. _____

_____

2. _____

_____

3. _____

_____

A   The Civil War ended in 1865 with the defeat of the Confederacy (the South) by the Union (the North). The Thirteenth Amendment to the United States Constitution was adopted in that same year: it abolished slavery in the United States. The 4 million slaves in the South were freed. In 1868, the Fourteenth Amendment was adopted, which made the former slaves citizens of the United States.

B   Though blacks were finally free U.S. citizens, their lives continued to be difficult. Since slaves had received little or no education, most free blacks could neither read nor write. There were not many jobs; most of the work in the South was in farming. To make things even harder, many Southern states passed laws that segregated, or separated, white and black people in schools, restaurants, on public transportation, and in other public places such as at phone booths and water fountains. These segregation laws would keep white and black people divided for many years. Wealthy whites also tried to stop blacks from voting in government elections. As U.S. citizens, blacks had the right to vote. But many Southern states used a literacy test, which white people didn't have to take, to stop blacks from voting. If a black person could not pass the test, he or she was not allowed to vote.

C   Life for Southern blacks did not improve until World War I (1914–1918) when thousands of blacks went north to look for jobs in factories that made war materials. More blacks migrated north for factory jobs during World War II (1939–1945), and a million black men and women served in the United States armed forces. When these soldiers returned from the war after fighting for the freedom of others, many wanted freedom at home. For blacks, this meant fighting the segregation laws that had been passed in the South after the Civil War. One civil rights organization, the National Association for the Advancement of Colored People (better known as the NAACP), fought the segregation laws in public schools. In 1954, in a case called 'Brown v. Board of Education,' the United States Supreme Court ruled that segregation in public schools was against the law. The next year the Supreme Court ordered all public schools to be desegregated—that is, the Court said that there could not be separate schools for blacks and whites and that all schools must be open to both.

D   In the same year, 1955, Rosa Parks, a 42-year-old seamstress, was arrested in Montgomery, Alabama. What was her crime? She had refused to give up her seat on a public bus to a white person. At that time in Alabama, segregation laws required blacks to give up their seats to whites and to sit in the back of the bus. Four days after Rosa Parks was put in jail, the black community in Montgomery, led by Dr. Martin Luther King, Jr., and other ministers, began a boycott of the city's buses. (Blacks refused to ride the city buses.) The boycott lasted 381 days. Dr. King and other leaders took Rosa Parks's case to the U.S. Supreme Court. The Court ruled that segregation on public buses was against the law. For her role in the boycott, Rosa Parks became known as the "mother of the civil rights movement."

E   In another famous incident, in 1960, four black college students in Greensboro, North Carolina, sat down to order lunch at a Woolworth store (a store that also had a small restaurant). Segregation laws at that time prohibited blacks from eating with whites. The Greensboro incident—called a sit-in—resulted in demonstrations all across the South. Demonstrators demanded an end to segregation in restaurants and other public places.

F   Perhaps the best known event of the civil rights movement was the March on Washington on August 28, 1963. Medgar Evers, the leader of the NAACP in Mississippi, was murdered by a white racist. Civil rights groups quickly organized a protest march. About 250,000 people, including approximately 50,000 whites, marched to the Lincoln Memorial in Washington, D.C. to demand jobs and freedom. At the end of the day, Dr. Martin Luther King, Jr., gave his famous "I have a dream" speech.

G   In 1968, Dr. King was killed by a white man. During his short life, he used non-violent action in the fight against discrimination. His speeches moved a nation. Today, many African Americans enjoy a middle-class life, but not all the problems have been solved, and new problems have developed. In inner-city neighborhoods, poverty, poor education, single-parent families, drugs, and crime destroy lives. On many college campuses, students associate only with members of their own racial group. In the workplace, whites are turning against affirmative-action policies which some people feel give special treatment to blacks. As this country moves into a new century, what will make it possible for all African Americans to participate in the American Dream? What can America do to unify its citizens?

After You Read

3. Make a Time Line   What were some important events in the fight for freedom and equality in the United States? On a separate sheet of paper, make a time line of events from the reading. The first event is done for you. When you finish, compare time lines with a partner.

1865

———▶

Thirteenth
Amendment
abolishes
slavery

4. Look for the Point of View   What is the author's point of view in "The Road to Freedom?" Is she for, against, or neutral toward the steps taken by African Americans and others to gain freedom and equality? Discuss these questions with a partner. Then share your answers in small groups.

5. Write and Discuss   Read **Just the Facts**. Then read the questions that
follow and write your answers on a separate sheet of paper. Discuss your answers
in small groups.

Just the Facts: African Americans

- For almost a century, many African Americans have moved from the South to the North and West of the United States. Today, some African Americans are moving to the South.

- The Museum of African American History opened in Detroit, Michigan, in 1997. It includes a slave ship with forty life-sized figures, which were modeled on African Americans living in Detroit.

SIGNS OF PROGRESS:
- In 1970, the high school dropout rate for African Americans was 27.9 percent. In 1990, it had fallen to 13.2 percent.
- In 1985, 26.1 percent of African American high school graduates from 18 to 24 years old were attending college. In 1990, the figure rose to 33 percent.
- In 1970, 10 percent of African Americans worked in professional or managerial jobs. In 1992, 16.8 percent did.

NO SIGNS OF PROGRESS:
- In 1972, the median income for African American households was about 58 percent that of white households. In 1992, it was about the same.

1. What do you think will happen to race relations in the United States in the next fifty years? Will the situation get better or worse? Why do you think so?
2. What is the image of African Americans presented in the media (movies, television, newspapers) today? Are African Americans presented fairly by the media?
3. Should the U.S. government apologize to African Americans for slavery? Should they be given compensation (money) for the way their ancestors were treated? Why or why not?

CHAPTER 11

Part One

Columbus's Voyage

Before You Read

1. Take a Quiz   What do you already know about Christopher Columbus? Work with a partner. Complete the following sentences by circling the letter of each correct answer.

---

1. Christopher Columbus was born in
    a. Spain.   **b.** Italy.
    c. Portugal.

2. Columbus wanted to sail to
    a. China, Japan, and other countries.
    b. India.
    c. North and South America.

3. Columbus sailed for the rulers of
    a. Spain.
    b. Italy.
    c. Portugal.

4. On his first voyage, he landed in
    a. Venezuela.   **b.** the Bahamas.
    c. Florida.

5. Columbus sailed to the Americas
    a. twice.
    b. three times.
    c. four times.

6. Columbus believed he had sailed to
    a. a new world.
    b. China, Japan, and other countries.
    c. India.

While You Read

2. Look for Answers   While you read "Columbus's Voyage" on pages 89 and 90, check your answers to the quiz items in Exercise 1. Make changes, if necessary. Then compare answers with a partner.

A   In 1451, Christopher Columbus was born in Genoa, Italy, on the coast of the Mediterranean Sea. At 14, he became a sailor. When he was 25, he was shipwrecked along the coast of Portugal. At that time, Portugal was the center of European exploration. Columbus stayed in Portugal for nine years, learning new navigational skills. He also gained experience on voyages to England, Ireland, Iceland, and the west coast of Africa. On one journey to Africa, Columbus heard reports of Africans wearing gold ornaments. He also heard that the Portuguese called West Africa the Gold Coast. Columbus's lifelong interest in gold began on these voyages.

B   In the late 1400s, the Muslim kingdoms of the Near East controlled the sea routes between Europe and Asia. But Columbus dreamed of finding a shorter unrestricted sea route to the silk, spices, and other treasures of the East. He wanted to try to reach the Indies by sailing west across the Atlantic. At that time, the term *the Indies* was used for China, Japan, Indonesia, Thailand, and the islands between those lands and India.

C   To make his voyage, Columbus needed ships and money. First, he asked King John II of Portugal, but the king rejected his proposal. The Portuguese were planning their own sea route to the Indies around the southern tip of Africa. Next, Columbus turned to Queen Isabella and King Ferdinand of Spain. They also refused. At that point, they were at war with the Muslims, called Moors, in Spain. But six years later, in 1492, the Christians defeated the Moors in Granada. Queen Isabella recognized the advantage of Columbus's idea of shorter routes to the Indies controlled by Spain, not by the Muslims. Columbus had also promised the queen gold and islands to rule. Later that year, the queen gave Columbus money for three ships.

D   Columbus and his sailors left Spain on August 3, 1492. Columbus kept two records of the journey—one for himself and another for his crew. In the crew's record, he lied about the distance traveled. He wanted his men to think the distance was less so they didn't feel so far from home. After almost ten weeks, the crew wanted to turn back, but Columbus refused. The sailors agreed to go on, but for only three more days. The next day, they saw signs of land: grass and wood in the water. Two days later, on October 12, they saw land. Columbus thought he was at the edge of the Indies, so he called the inhabitants Indians. (They were members of the Arawak tribe.) He described them as friendly, gentle people carrying spears. However, he had landed not in the Indies, but on an island in what is now the Bahamas.

E   Columbus then sailed south to what is now Cuba, Haiti, and the Dominican Republic. When one of the ships, the Santa Maria, hit some coral reefs, the crew used the wood from the destroyed ship to build a fort. Columbus left forty men with the fort. Then he headed back to Spain with the two remaining ships, the Niña and the Pinta, filled with plants, animals, and "Indians" from "the Indies." He arrived back in Spain on April 14, 1493.

F $\}$ Columbus made three more voyages to the New World—to Cuba later in 1493, to Trinidad and the coast of Venezuela in 1498, and to Honduras, Nicaragua, and Panama in 1502. After four journeys, he still believed he had reached the Indies. Although he was mistaken, his voyage, for better or for worse, changed the world.

After You Read

3. Draw the Sea Routes   Work with a partner. Use information from the reading to draw lines showing Columbus's four voyages. Mark each route with the date of the voyage.

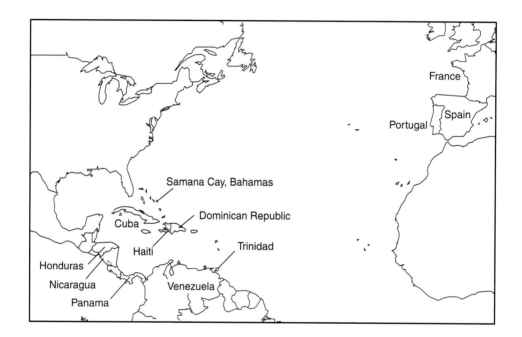

4. Complete the Conversation Use words from the box to complete the conversation. Compare answers with a partner.

---

crew   described   fort   inhabitants   journey   land   ✓sailed   ship   voyages   west

---

MAX: Why isn't there a Herjulfsson Day instead of a Columbus Day?

RICK: What are you talking about? Who is Her . . . Her . . . What was that name?

MAX: Bjarni Herjulfsson, a Norwegian who _____sailed_____[1] to the Americas hundreds of years before Columbus. He was on a _____[2] to Greenland but was blown to Newfoundland or Labrador in a storm. He and his crew saw _____[3] but never got off their _____.[4]

RICK: You mean Columbus wasn't the first European to reach the Americas?

MAX: No. He wasn't even the second. In the year 1000, Leif Eriksson sailed _____[5] from Greenland in search of the land Herjulfsson had _____.[6] He and his _____[7] spent the winter there. In 1010, others followed and built a _____[8] there, but after a while the _____[9] drove them away.

RICK: Do you think Columbus heard about those early _____[10]?

MAX: Who knows?

RICK: Well, in any case, who could pronounce that guy's name?

5. Write and Discuss On a separate sheet of paper, write your answers to the following questions. Then discuss your opinions in small groups.

1. Why do you think Leif Eriksson and other early explorers have been forgotten and Columbus is remembered?
2. What does "Columbus's Voyage" tell you about Columbus the man? Use details from the reading to support your opinion.
3. What similarities are there between Columbus's voyage and space travel today?
4. Imagine you are Columbus. Try to convince Queen Isabella to support your plan to find a shorter route to the Indies. Working with a partner, write a short conversation between the queen and Columbus. Then act out your conversation for the class.

Part Two

Five Hundred Years Later

Before You Read

1. Discuss   In small groups, discuss the following question: Should the United States have celebrated the five hundredth anniversary of Columbus's voyage? Why or why not? Share your group's opinions with the class.

While You Read

2. Describe a Drawing for Each Paragraph   Think about a drawing that would illustrate the most important idea in each paragraph of the reading on pages 93 and 94. Describe each drawing below. Then compare answers with a partner.

Paragraph A: _____

Paragraph B: _____

Paragraph C: _____

Paragraph D: _Native Americans protesting at a Columbus Day celebration_____

Paragraph E: _____

Paragraph F: _____

Paragraph G: _____

Paragraph H: _____

A   In 1992, Spain, Italy, and the United States celebrated the five hundredth anniversary of Columbus's voyage to the Americas. Spain and Italy organized elaborate festivities. In the United States, the anniversary was, for many people, a reason to celebrate, but for others it was a reason to protest.

B   Spain spent 20 billion dollars on its festivities. The city of Seville held an international fair. In Barcelona, an artist arranged the marriage of Christopher Columbus to Lady Liberty—using statues, of course. Genoa, Italy, spent 650 million dollars on an exhibit called "Christopher Columbus: Ships and the Sea."

C   In the United States, the annual Columbus Day parades were larger than usual. In New York City, Italian Americans celebrated with a huge parade up Fifth Avenue. Hispanic Americans in New York celebrated by holding a separate Hispanic heritage parade. These and other parades marked the start of a year of Columbus conferences and commemorations.

D   Native Americans, on the other hand, did not celebrate the five hundredth anniversary; many protested. Columbus is no hero to them. In New York City, someone poured red paint on a statue of Columbus, and another protester walked along the Fifth Avenue parade with a placard that said, "This Land Was Stolen, Not Discovered." In North Stonington, Connecticut, Native Americans gathered for an anti-Columbus Day. In Los Angeles, Native Americans in bright headdresses and war paint protested at a shelter for homeless Native Americans. Around the country, many Native Americans wore black armbands to protest the day.

E   The anniversary provided an opportunity to look back at the man and his legacy. Columbus's life—both the positive and negative aspects—was the topic of several conferences, articles, and books. While Columbus became an extraordinary sea captain, he was not without flaws. He had a vision, but he was driven by an obsession with gold and fame. He was a skillful navigator, but he nearly lost control of his crew on his first voyage. He completed four voyages, surviving fierce winter storms, but he was mistaken in his belief that he had reached the Indies when, in fact, he was still thousands of miles away. In the end, he was a cruel colonial administrator. He and other crew members treated the Indians cruelly, capturing, torturing, and killing many of them.

F To Native Americans, Columbus and the Europeans who followed were invaders who robbed them of their land, their language, and their culture. These European invaders also brought disease, torture, and slavery to many Native Americans. In their view, the destruction of Native American civilization began with Columbus's arrival.

G Clearly, many of the explorers and early settlers acted with great cruelty, but cruel behavior was not new in the Americas. The Aztecs and Mayans of Mexico practiced human sacrifice and held slaves. The Caribe Indians in the Caribbean islands were cannibals. And North American Indians such as the Apache, Sioux, and Iroquois were known as fierce warriors and were feared by their neighbors.

H The world was very different in Columbus's time. To judge it by today's standards would mean ignoring that reality. Whatever one's point of view about Columbus, the anniversary—with its celebrations, discussions, and protests—gave us the opportunity to look at Columbus anew.

After You Read

3. React to the Reading   On a separate sheet of paper, write your reaction to something that surprised or interested you in the reading. Then, in small groups, share your reactions.

4. Look for the Point of View   What is the author's point of view in "Five Hundred Years Later"? Is she for, against, or neutral about celebrating the anniversary of Columbus's voyage? How do you know? Discuss this question with a partner. Then share your answers in small groups.

Review Strategy

If you want to review something you have read, look through each paragraph. Find words that tell you the topic of the paragraph, and write them down on a separate sheet of paper. Here is an example: 500th anniversary of Columbus's voyage
celebrate
protest

---

5. Look for Examples   Read the following points of view. Then find examples in the reading to support each point of view. Compare answers with a partner.

1.   Columbus was an extraordinary man. He should be remembered for his historic voyages.

_____

_____

2.   Columbus was a flawed man who brought cruelty to the American Indians.

_____

_____

3.   The destruction of American Indian culture started with Columbus.

_____

_____

6. Write and Discuss   Read **Just the Facts**. Then read the questions that follow and write your answers on a separate sheet of paper. Discuss your answers in small groups.

Just the Facts: Columbus

- Columbus was the oldest of five children in a family of wool weavers.
- Columbus married a Portuguese woman who died eight years before his first voyage. Some historians believe he abandoned her. Columbus had a son, Diego, with his wife, and a second son, Ferdinand, with his Spanish mistress.
- After Columbus's voyage, the Americas were believed to be part of Asia. By 1520, the Americas were considered to be a "New World." But it wasn't until the 1700s that the Americas were proved to be separate from Asia.
- The District of Columbia (Washington, D.C.) was named for Christopher Columbus.
- Columbus Day is a legal holiday in many states. It is celebrated on the second Monday in October. It used to be celebrated on October 12.

1.   What is your opinion of Columbus based on the two readings in this chapter and the facts above?
2.   The American writer Ralph Waldo Emerson (1803–1882) wrote: "The most advanced nations are always those who navigate the most." Do you agree? Why or why not?
3.   What should the United States do for the six hundredth anniversary of Columbus's voyage?

CHAPTER 12

Part One

The First Americans

Before You Read

1. Discuss   In small groups, discuss the following questions: Who were the first people to live in your country thousands of years ago? How were they treated by groups that came later?

While You Read

2. Write Captions   Use information from "Who Were the First Americans?"on pages 97 and 98 to write captions (descriptions) under the drawings below. Compare captions with a partner.

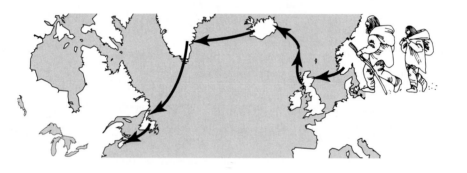

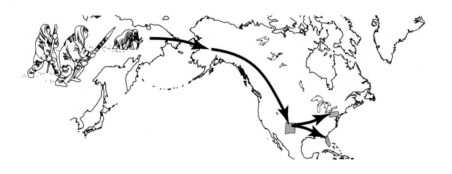

A The Americas were a "New World" to the European explorers of the fifteenth and sixteenth centuries. But, in fact, people had lived in the Americas for at least seventeen thousand years before Columbus arrived. Who were these first Americans?

B For a long time, archaeological evidence has pointed to Asians from Siberia as the first migrants to the Americas. These Asians hunted large animals, such as the mammoth. They probably followed these animals across a land bridge from Siberia to what is now Alaska. Today, a body of water, the Bering Strait, separates the two lands. But during the Ice Age, frigid temperatures froze much of the seas into glaciers, lowering sea levels about 350 feet. This drop in sea levels created a land bridge that connected the continents of Asia and North America. Many archaeologists believe that this first migration happened about seventeen thousand years ago. However, fossilized bone tools have been found in Alaska. These tools suggest that humans have been in the Americas for at least twenty-seven thousand years.

C After the Asian hunters reached Alaska, glaciers probably stopped them from moving south and east. But fifteen thousand years ago, the climate warmed and melted the glaciers. The descendants of the Asian hunters spread out over North and South America. The evidence of their movement in the New World is in the weapons, tools, and baskets they left behind in present-day New Mexico, Pennsylvania, Florida, and elsewhere. The weapons (spears with stone points used for killing large animals) are approximately twelve thousand years old. They are called Clovis points because they were first found in Clovis, New Mexico. The mammoth hunters who used them are called Clovis people.

D About five thousand years ago, other groups of Asian migrants came to the Americas. They were Eskimos (also called Inuits) and Aleuts, who crossed the Bering Strait by boat.

E Recent archaeological evidence suggests, however, that the earliest migrants may have been people from Europe, not Asia. According to one theory, these Europeans migrated through Asia, then walked over the land bridge from Siberia to Alaska. According to another theory, the Europeans walked over land and a series of ice bridges from France or Scandinavia to Scotland, to the Faeroe Islands (between Great Britain and Iceland), to Iceland, to Greenland, and finally to Canada.

F   Two types of evidence support the view that the earliest Americans were from Europe. First, seven human skeletons which are from eight to eleven thousand years old have been found in North America. All of the skulls have some European characteristics. Some of these skeletons have been compared with groups from around the world. They do not resemble modern Native Americans. They do, however, resemble the Ainu of Japan—a group that had wavy hair, full beards, and other European characteristics. The second type of evidence comes from the early migrants' technology—a particular way of making tools and weapons. Tools and weapons like those made by the Clovis people have been found in Europe, but not in Asia. If the first migrants were from Europe, they were probably replaced by a later group of Asians. These later migrants are the ancestors of today's Native Americans.

G   Research on the first Americans has now become more difficult. Native American groups have argued that researchers are stealing bones from their ancestors' graves to put in museums. Taking bones from graves is against Native American tribal traditions. A law was passed in 1990 to stop this practice. This law requires the United States government to return to Native Americans any bones that are believed to have belonged to their ancestors so that the tribe can rebury them. Two of the oldest skeletons have already been returned and reburied. But researchers say that if skeletons are returned, the history of the earliest Americans will be buried with the bones. And, researchers ask, if skeletons have European characteristics, are they really the ancestors of today's Native Americans? Researchers are trying to recover another skeleton, called Kennewick Man, that was returned to Native Americans. The United States Supreme Court may have to decide who has the right to this and other skeletons. For now, there is still no definite answer to the question: "Who were the first Americans?"

After You Read

3. Mark the Text   Reread the story and mark the main idea of each paragraph by writing "MI" in the margin. The main idea is the most important point of the paragraph. It's what the author says about the topic. For example, the main idea of paragraph A is:

> MI: people had lived in the Americas for at least seventeen thousand years before Columbus arrived

Then compare answers with a partner.

4. Write a Summary   Look at what you marked in Exercise 3 for the main idea of each paragraph. Write a summary of the entire reading in your own words on a separate sheet of paper. Then read your summary to your partner. Ask your partner for his or her reactions to your summary. Make changes to your summary, if necessary.

5. Identify Stated or Implied Information   Some information is stated directly in the story. Other information is implied; it is not stated directly. Details in the story suggest that it's true. Work with a partner. Write *stated* or *implied* next to each statement below.

EXAMPLE: _____ *stated* _____ Eskimos and Aleuts crossed the Bering Strait by boat.

_____ *implied* _____ When the Eskimos came five thousand years ago, the glaciers had melted and separated the two continents.

_____ **1.** Fossilized bone tools that are twenty-seven thousand years old were found in Alaska.

_____ **2.** Humans made the bone tools found in Alaska.

_____ **3.** The Clovis people were skilled hunters.

_____ **4.** The Clovis people used spears with stone points to kill large animals.

_____ **5.** There are two theories about how European people came to America.

_____ **6.** The evidence that European people were the first Americans comes from their skeletons, and how they made their tools and weapons.

_____ **7.** The law passed in 1990 supports Native Americans, not the reseachers.

6. Write and Discuss   On a separate sheet of paper, write your answers to the following questions. Then discuss your opinions in small groups.

1. Who do you support in the fight over skeletons: the Native Americans or the researchers? Why?

2. Someday, if evidence proves that the first Americans were Europeans, how will this affect the group now called Native Americans?

The Native American Story: A Struggle for Survival

Before You Read

1. Discuss In small groups, discuss the following question: What do you already know about the history and current life of Native Americans (also called American Indians)?

While You Read

2. Make an Outline Make an outline of the most important points in each paragraph of the reading on pages 101 and 102. When you finish, compare outlines with a partner. Do you agree on the important points?

The Native American Story: A Struggle for Survival

Paragraph A: _____

_____

Paragraph B: _____

_____

Paragraph C: _____

_____

Paragraph D: _____

_____

Paragraph E: _____

_____

Paragraph F: _____

_____

Paragraph G: _____

_____

Paragraph H: _____

_____

A   When the European explorers arrived in the Americas in the late 1400s and early 1500s, the American Indian population of North America was between 7 and 12 million. Over a period of five hundred years, contact with Europeans and their descendants has decimated the native peoples. Today, the American Indian (Native American) population in the United States is only 2 million.

B   Life for the native peoples changed disastrously with the arrival of Europeans. Many American Indians died in battles over land. But many more died from diseases the Europeans brought with them, such as smallpox, measles, influenza, and the plague.

C   Once the British colonies became an independent country—the United States—the situation became worse for American Indians. As American settlers began exploring and settling in the land west of the Mississippi River, American Indian tribes lost their hunting lands and, with it, their way of life. When gold was discovered in California in 1848, one hundred thousand people from the eastern United States migrated over Indian lands in search of gold. When Indian tribes resisted this invasion, the U.S. government sent in troops to open the way.

D   Over the next half century, government policies took away much of the Indians' remaining land. The government forced tribes onto reservations by 1876 and then reduced the size of the reservations. Many of the Indians on the Great Plains had been hunters. With their hunting grounds gone, they were forced to become farmers on the often poor lands of the reservations. In the late 1800s, U.S. government policies were based on the prediction that the Indians would not survive. By the early 1900s, a survey did indeed show that the remaining Native Americans were suffering badly from poverty, unemployment, little education, poor health, and alcoholism. But they proved the government wrong. They did survive and, by the 1930s, their population finally began to increase. Other changes followed.

E   Starting in the 1960s during the civil rights movement, Native American groups took important steps to improve their lives and bring about a rebirth of their people. They promoted an American Indian identity and renewed pride in their culture. A flood of Indian newspapers, magazines, and books were published, reaching people both inside and outside the reservations.

F   In 1968, Congress passed the Civil Rights Act, which returned to the tribes the right to use their own tribal laws on the reservations. The same year, the American Indian Movement, called AIM, was established by the Chippewa Indians. AIM demanded new economic and educational opportunities. Since then, special Indian tribal colleges have been established, and Native American languages are being taught in public schools in different parts of the country. For example, Mohawk is taught in upstate New York, Lakota in South Dakota, and Kickapoo in Oklahoma. Alaskan native peoples have managed to regain 40 million acres of their land. They have also been compensated almost one billion dollars by the government for their losses. And the Native American Rights Fund (NARF) has taken back from the government thousands of acres of land along the Atlantic Coast.

G   In the early 1980s, some Native American communities came up with an unusual way to better themselves—they opened gambling casinos on their reservations. More than fifty tribes have followed their example. The casinos that have been successful create jobs, and the profits pay for health care, college tuition, and new homes for those living on the reservations.

H   By the end of the nineteenth century, Native Americans were suffering from many problems and appeared to be headed for extinction. By the end of the twentieth century, although many problems remain, there have been a number of developments that offer hope. At least two important questions need to be answered, however. Do Native Americans need to remain a separate nation within the United States to survive and flourish? And will the larger society see that as the best solution for this centuries-old conflict?

After You Read

3. React to the Reading   On a separate sheet of paper, write your reaction to something that surprised or interested you in the reading. Then, in small groups, share your reactions.

4. Look for the Point of View   What is the author's point of view in the reading? Is she more sympathetic to the Native Americans or to the European settlers and the U.S. government? How do you know? Discuss these questions with a partner. Then share your answers in small groups.

5. Make an Argument If you wanted to write a letter to convince the U.S. government to improve the lives of Native Americans, what would you say? Use details from this chapter and any other relevant details to make an argument. Write a draft and read it to your partner. Ask your partner for his or her reactions. Make changes to your letter, if necessary.

6. Write and Discuss Read **Just the Facts**. Then read the questions that follow and write your answers on a separate sheet of paper. Discuss your answers in small groups.

Just the Facts: Native Americans

- Native Americans were given U.S. citizenship in 1924.
- American Indian families earn only one-third as much as the average family in the United States.
- The suicide rate among Native American teenagers is ten times the U.S. average.
- The states with the largest Native American populations are:

  1. Oklahoma (252,000)
  2. California (242,000)
  3. Arizona (204,000)
  4. New Mexico (134,000)
  5. Alaska (86,000)

- The largest American Indian tribes (in 1990) were the Navajo and the Cherokee.
- The largest reservations (in 1990) were: The Navajo (in Arizona, New Mexico, and Utah), Pine Ridge (in Nebraska and South Dakota), and Fort Apache (in Arizona).
- In 1990, about 437,000 Native Americans were living on reservations and trust lands (lands owned by the U.S. government outside the reservation).

1. Do you think it's important to teach Native American languages in public schools with large numbers of Native Americans? Why or why not?

2. Are gambling casinos on reservations a good way to improve life on the reservations? Why or why not?

3. What images of Native Americans are part of popular culture in the United States? For example, how are Native Americans usually portrayed in movies? What do you think of these portrayals?

Unit Four

In Unit Four, you read about some aspects of the history of two minority groups in the United States: African Americans and Native Americans. Based on what you have read, has your attitude toward these groups changed? Has your attitude toward people in the U.S. changed?

1. Discuss Your Feelings Write some sentences that describe your feelings about the people you read about in this unit. You may choose some of these phrases to begin your sentences or use others of your own.

> I was surprised to learn . . .
> I didn't know that . . .
> I can't understand/believe why/. . .
> I wonder why . . .

In small groups, discuss your sentences. How are your feelings similar? How are they different?

2. Evaluate This Book Now that you have finished this book, think about the exercises and strategies that helped you the most. In small groups, discuss the following questions.

1. Which exercises helped you to understand the readings?
2. Which exercises helped you to remember information that you read?
3. Which exercises helped you learn new words and expressions?
4. Which strategies helped you the most with your English?

Continue to use these exercises and strategies as you learn English!

Follow-Up

You can learn more about these topics by doing research and reporting information to your class. You can also read books and watch movies about these topics. Here are some suggestions.

Chapter 10
Video Series. The following video series are available through the Public Broadcasting Service (PBS), which operates public television stations across the United States. They are also available in many public libraries in the United States.
The Civil War, a 9-part documentary, produced by Ken Burns
Eyes on the Prize, a 14-hour documentary on the history of the civil rights movement

Chapter 11
Movie. *Conquest of Paradise*, a 1992 drama starring Gerard Depardieu and Sigourney Weaver

Chapter 12
Movie. *Dances with Wolves*, a 1990 drama, starring Kevin Costner

Answer Key

CHAPTER 1 **Part One** 2. 1. b, 2. c, 3. a 4. 1. b, 2. c, 3. a 5. 2 6. 1. company-It 2. new products-These 3. Hallmark-It 4. greeting cards-them 7. (from top to bottom) 6, 3, 1, 4, 2, 5 8. 2. wrapping, 3. ribbon, 4. postcards, 5. keep in touch **Part Two** 1. 2. Be My Valentine! 1. Have a Very Merry Christmas! 4. Is he husband number 3 or 4? 3. You're 20 with 30 years of experience. Happy Birthday! 3. 1. Each year, people in the United States buy more than seven billion cards. 2. Simple: They present a beautiful picture on the cover and cheerful words inside. Complex: They can have a strange photograph on the outside and a funny joke inside. Some birthday cards play an electronic musical message, and some Valentine's Day cards fill the air with perfume. 3. Because of the high rate of divorce and second marriages in the United States, there are now anniversary cards for "Mom and her husband" and "Dad and his wife." Now there are cards for the person who lost a job, lost a game, or lost some weight. 4. 2 5. 1. d, 2. e, 3. a, 4. c, 5. b 7. 1. produce, 2. photographs, 4. messages, 5. buy, 6. quick

CHAPTER 2 **Part One** 2. 1. c, 2. a, 3. d, 4. b 4. According to the reading: The Barbie doll represents a limited and unrealistic standard of beauty. Cost is also a problem, because girls want several Barbie dolls. 5. 1. She has been the focus of a movie, an Andy Warhol painting, many photography exhibits, books, and a museum. 2. Since 1959, the manufacturer has produced nearly a billion Barbie dolls. Children and adults collect the doll. A typical girl in the U.S. owns eight Barbie dolls. She has been the focus of a movie, an Andy Warhol painting, many photography exhibits, books, and a museum. 6. 1. b, 2. d, 3. a, 4. c 7. 1. b, 2. c, 3. e, 4. a, 5. d 9. (from top to bottom) 3, 1, 4, 2, 5 10. 1. THE ARTS: movies, paintings, photography, books, plays, dance, music, sculpture 2. CAREERS: toy manufacturer, fashion model, doctor, astronaut, paleontologist, artist, actor, photographer, writer 3. PEOPLE: sister, boyfriend, friends, girls, adults, parents, Andy Warhol (and all the careers in category 2) **Part Two** 2. Evidence that the G.I. Joe doll can teach boys to be violent: The doll says: "Attack! Eat lead, Cobra!" Evidence that the Barbie doll can teach girls to focus too much on clothes and weddings: The doll says: "Let's go shopping!" and "Let's plan our dream wedding!" 6. 1. d, 2. a, 3. c, 4. b, 5. e 7. 3 8. 1. This parent is for the Barbie doll. 2. This parent is against the Barbie doll. 10. 1. dolls, 2. message, 3. altered, 4. stereotypes, 5. parent, 6. children

CHAPTER 3 **Part One** 1. 1. lasso, 2. stagecoach robbery, 3. branding iron, 4. riding a bronco, 5. roping a calf, 6. cattle drive 2. a. The cowboy symbolizes freedom and adventure. b. News of the cowboy spread with the help of dime novels, especially The Virginian, and the play, movies, and television shows based on it. 4. 1. b, 2. d, 3. a, 4. c 5. 3 6. 1. got together, 2. cattle drive, 3. adventure, 4. ride, 5. lasso, 6. went wild **Part Two** 1. 1. Possible predictions: today's cowboys, television cowboys, rodeos, sculpture of Native Americans, art of the west 2. 1. d, 2. b, 3. c, 4. a 4. 3 5. (from top to bottom) 3, 5, 1, 6, 4, 2 6. 1. a cowboy museum, 2. a rodeo, 3. a cowboy museum, 4. a village museum, 5. a rodeo, 6. a village museum 7. 1 8. 1. prairie, 2. on the road, 3. rodeo, 4. living, 5. simpler, 6. cowboy

CHAPTER 4 **Part One** 1. 1. Egypt, 2. Korea, 3. Mexico, 4. Poland 2. 1. c, 3. b, 4. d, 5. a 3. 1 5. 4, 6, 2, 5, 1, 3 6. 1. consisted of thirteen states. 2. there were twenty states. 3. the country grew from twenty states to fifty states. 4. the United States has continued to consist of fifty states. 7. 2. Day, 3. symbolize, 4. flag **Part Two** 1. 1. d, 2. a, 3. b 2. 1. f, 2. e, 3. c. No matching picture: a, b, and d. 4. 1. To some, especially veterans, the flag is a symbol of patriotism. To others, it represents traditional values. To others, it's a symbol of freedom, including the right to use the flag for everything from painting to politics. 2. art: Jasper Johns painted the flag several times. fashion: fashion designers have created flag shirts, flag ties, flag jackets, flag shoes, and even flag bikinis. Young people have worn flags on their clothes to protest or to support patriotism. food: Bakers make flag cakes for the Fourth of July. 3. Some burn the flag to protest government policies. 5. A country's flag is its most common symbol. A symbol, however, can mean different things to different people. 6. 1. shirts, ties, jackets, shoes, bikinis 2. States: Alaska, Hawaii, California, New York, Florida 3. artist, fashion designer, baker, secretary, doctor 4. veterans, young people, political groups, Americans, the Supreme Court 7. 2. Patriotism, 3. wear, 4. died, 5. fought, 6. flag

CHAPTER 5 **Part One** 2. 1. b, 2. c, 3. e, 4. a 3. The design of the White House was not original. It was partly based on Leinster House in Dublin, Ireland. James Hoban, the Irish immigrant who designed the White House, would have seen this building before he left Ireland. 4. 1792: James Hoban won a contest for the best design for the president's house. 1800: The construction of the president's house was completed. 1814: The president's mansion was burned during a war with the British. (Or: Dolley Madison saved a painting and many documents from a fire in the White House.) 1902: The 'White House' became the official name for the president's house. 5. 1. official, 2. rooms, 3. President, 4. works, 5. painting 6. official = approved or authorized by the government **Part Two** 2. A: A collage of Washington buildings and monuments, including: the White House, the Washington Monument, the Jefferson Memorial, and the Lincoln Memorial. B. A sculpture of FDR from the memorial in Washington, D.C. C. A drawing of FDR surrounded by people building schools and roads, and planting trees in parks during the Great Depression. D. A drawing of the elaborate FDR Memorial next to a simple plaque with FDR's name on it. 4. monument in Washington, D.C., of the twentieth century, crisis known as the Great Depression, people in the United States, in 1997, many people were happy, but not everybody. 5. 1. for example, the monuments and memorials to Washington, Jefferson, Lincoln, and now FDR. 2. such as building schools and roads, planting trees, and creating parks. 3. different groups complained about the high cost of the memorial, a sculpture of the First Lady wearing a fur, sculptures of the president without any wheelchair, a monument to the high levels of government spending under FDR, and the fact that this was not the simple plaque that FDR wanted. 6. 1. d, 2. a, 3. c, 4. b

CHAPTER 6 **Part One** 1. b, 2. c, 3. d, 4. a 3. 1812 → 1812 to 1814 → 1914 to 1918 → 1961 4. 1 5. (the last sentence) . . . the name Uncle Sam came from the friendly meat man, Sam Wilson. 6. 1. nickname, 2. symbol, 3. every, 4. war, 5. says, 6. many, 7. stripes, 8. country **Part Two** 1. 1. a, 2. b, 3. a, 4. b, 5. b, 6. b 4. Late 1700s: 13, agricultural, 2 million, Britain and Africa. Today: 50, service, 260 million, many countries 5. 1. when the war took place 2. the definition of 'suburbs' 6. 1. a manufacturing economy - workers make products, such as cars or computers 2. a service economy - workers provide a service, such as cooking or consulting 3. downsized - making their workforce smaller 7. 1. fact, 2. opinion, 3. opinion, 4. fact, 5. opinion **Unit Two** 1. j, 2. h, 3. f, 4. a, 5. g, 6. b, 7. i, 8. c, 9. d, 10. e

CHAPTER 7 **Part One** 2. 1. c, 2. a, 3. b 4. 1. Elite institutions which maintain the upper class, the way to top jobs, a way to gain prestige through a diploma. 2. half of the students receive financial aid; they are no longer all-male; students come from all races, religious groups, and social classes 3. Graduates are still expected to make annual cash donations. 5. 1. fact, 2. opinion, 3. opinion, 4. fact, 5. fact 6. 1. Yale . . . Dartmouth . . . Cornell 2. 1701 . . . 1769 . . . 1853 3. Protestant 7. 1. name, 2. gifts, 3. graduates' 8. 2. graduates, 3. established, 4. women, 5. institutions **Part Two** 1. b, 2. b, 3. b, 4. a, 5. a 4. 1. B, 2. A, E, 3. E, 4. - , 5. D, 6. C 5. 2 6. 1. read his book Democracy in America. 2. enroll in a community college. 3. try to get more donations from alumni and corporations. 7. 1. home, 2. African, 3. century, 4. nationwide, 5. public, 6. practical, 7. work, 8. goals

CHAPTER 8 **Part One**   2. 1. . . . was one of America's leading architects of the 20th century. 3. . . . focused on comfort, convenience, and open spaces. 4. . . . remained standing after an earthquake destroyed Tokyo. 5. . . . in New York City was designed in the shape of a seashell. 6. . . . was designed by Wright in 1958, but wasn't built until recently. 5. His designs were non-traditional. They were different from what people were used to. Some people didn't like the inexpensive, mass-produced materials he used. 6. 1. He had an influence on architecture throughout the twentieth century. 2. These include the Frank Lloyd Wright House, the Dana House, and the Robie House. 3. Instead of the traditional design of a house, he created a flow of space. He used inexpensive materials. His designs were low and horizontal like the flat Mid-western landscape. 4. In the 1950s, construction of Wright's Convention Center was blocked by his opponents. It was recently built, and reactions have been mixed. 7. 2. influenced, 3. design, 4. space, 5. architect, 6. own, 7. influence **Part Two**   2. A: . . .one city has led the rest in architecture that is new in both form and function. B. a fire C. a building boom D. the tallest building and most modern architecture E. Why build such huge towers? 3. 1. b, 2. a, 3. f, 4. c, 5. e, 6. d 4. 1

CHAPTER 9 **Part One**   2. B. People leaving the Dust Bowl with all their belongings. C. Woody Guthrie on a freight train with his guitar and harmonica. D. Sheet music of Guthrie's songs. E. Guthrie recording a record album in a studio in New York. F. African Americans and whites holding hands and singing a song during a demonstration. G. A group of folksingers, including Bob Dylan, Joan Baez, Judy Collins, Richie Havens, and Arlo Guthrie. 4. 1. stated, 2. stated, 3. implied, 4. implied, 5. stated 5. 1. folk, 2. popular, 3. business, 4. influenced, 5. songwriters, 6. classics **Part Two**   1. b, 2. a, 3. a, 4. b, 5. a, 6. a 5. The author is probably against techno music. In paragraph A, she says that Guthrie would be shocked and disappointed by techno music. In paragraph E, she notes that techno-heads don't care about the problems of the poor, and she calls them pleasure seekers. In paragraph F, the author raises many questions which have a negative tone. 6. 1. b, 2. f, 3. -, 4. a, 5. d, 6. e, 7. c, 8. - 7. 1. go to a rave and dance to techno music. 2. turn on some ambient music. 3. produce your own techno music. **Unit Three**   1. c, 2. d, 3. b, 4. c, 5. a, 6. b, 7. d, 8. d

CHAPTER 10 **Part One**   2. The main causes were 1. states' rights vs. the federal government's rights, and 2. the spread of slavery. Other issues included: 1. how to help businesses that were struggling because of an economic depression. 2. the decision to dismiss the Dred Scott case. 3. Congressmen started voting with their region—North or South, instead of their political party. 4. Lincoln's election which provoked South Carolina to secede because Lincoln had promised to abolish slavery. 5. South Carolina's secession encouraged other Southern states to leave the Union and form the Confederate States of America. 4. Slavery in new states: North - against it; South - for it; Movement of property in new territories: North - This was an issue for the federal government to decide. South - This was an issue for the states to decide. The breakup of the Union: North - against the breakup; South - for it. 5. 1. national; 2. owning people who must work without pay, 3. end, 4. people who wanted to end slavery, 5. taxes, 6. leave (the Union) 6. 1. abolitionist, 3. slavery, 4. slaves, 5. freedom, 6. died, 7. North **Part Two**   2. 1. Dr. King speaking at the March on Washington in 1963. 2. Southern states used a literacy test to stop blacks from voting. 3. A million blacks served in the armed forces during World War II. 3. 1868: 14th Amendment made former slaves citizens → 1914: blacks moved north for jobs during World War I → 1939: a million blacks served in World War II → 1954: NAACP won Brown v. Board of Education → 1955: Rosa Parks's actions triggered a boycott of Montgomery's buses → 1960: Greensboro, North Carolina sit-in → 1963: March on Washington. 4. While the reading mainly presents, in neutral terms, the history of the struggle for freedom , no arguments are made against freedom for blacks. Also, some words indicate that the author is for this movement. For example, in referring to Rosa Parks's actions, the author asks somewhat sarcastically: "What was her crime?" The answer is that she refused to give up her seat on a bus to a white person. Also, the term "white racist" is used to describe the man who murdered Medgar Evers. And, in referring to Dr. King's fight against discrimination, the author states "His speeches moved a nation." This indicates a positive point of view toward the civil rights movement.

Chapter 11 **Part One**   1. 1. b, 2. a, 3. a, 4. b, 5. c, 6. b 3. 1492 - 1493: Bahamas, Cuba, Haiti, Dominican Republic; 1493: Cuba; 1498: Trinidad and Venezuela; 1502: Honduras, Nicaragua, Panama 4. 2. journey, 3. land, 4. ship, 5. west, 6. described, 7. crew, 8. fort, 9. inhabitants, 10. voyages **Part Two**   2. A: Some celebrating, others protesting the 500th anniversary of Columbus's voyage. 4. The author's point of view is neutral. She presents both sides: the point of view of those who celebrated the anniversary and those who protested it. She also presents both sides, of Columbus, the man. 5. 1. He had a vision and followed his dream. He was a skillful navigator and sea captain. He made four voyages during which he survived terrible winter storms. 2. Columbus was driven by his obsession with gold and fame. He almost lost control of his crew on one voyage. And, after four voyages, he still didn't know where he had landed, believing he had reached the Indies. He and his crew captured, tortured, and killed many Indians. They also brought disease and slavery to the Native Americans. Finally, Columbus was a cruel colonial administrator. 3. Columbus and those who followed took Native American land, and robbed the Indians of their language and their culture. They also brought disease, torture, and slavery to the Americas.

CHAPTER 12 **Part One**   2. Top picture: Recent evidence suggests that the first Americans migrated from Europe to Canada. Bottom picture: According to the standard theory, Asians from Siberia followed large animals across a land bridge to Alaska. 3. B. MI: evidence has pointed to Asians from Siberia as the first migrants to the Americas. . . . about seventeen thousand years ago. However, fossilized bone tools . . . suggest that humans have been in the Americas for at least twenty-seven thousand years. C. MI: But fifteen thousand years ago . . . The descendants of the Asian hunters spread out over North and South America. The evidence . . . is in the weapons, tools, and baskets they left behind. D. MI: About five thousand years ago, other groups of Asian migrants . . . crossed the Bering Strait by boat. E. MI: Recent archaeological evidence suggests...that the earliest migrants may have been people from Europe, not Asia. F. MI: Two types of evidence support the view that the earliest Americans were from Europe. . .seven human skeletons . . . have been found in North America. All . . . have some European characteristics. The second type of evidence comes from the early migrants' technology . . . Tools and weapons like those made by the Clovis people have been found in Europe, but not in Asia. G. MI: Research on the first Americans has now become more difficult. . .A law was passed in 1990 . . . requires the United States government to return to Native Americans any bones that are believed to have belonged to their ancestors . . . Researchers ask, if skeletons have European characteristics, are they really the ancestors of today's Native Americans? . . . For now, there is still no definite answer to the question: "Who were the first Americans?" 5. 1. implied, 2. implied, 3. implied, 4. stated, 5. stated, 6. stated, 7. implied **Part Two**   2. A: late 1400s-early 1500s: 7-12 million Native Americans (NAs) in North America. After 500 years with Europeans, only 2 million NAs in U.S. 4. The author is more sympathetic to the Native Americans. Her choice of words shows this, for example: "contact with Europeans . . . has decimated the native peoples." "Life for the native peoples changed disastrously with the arrival of Europeans." ". . . the situation became worse for American Indians." Only the Native Americans' side is presented, not the point of view of the Europeans or the U.S. government. The changes described, starting in the 1930s, have an optimistic tone. The author says a number of developments offer hope.